ADVANCED HOME WIRING

Current with Codes through 2014

**DC Circuits • Transfer Switches • Panel Upgrades
Circuit Maps • Much More**

Creative Publishing
international

MINNEAPOLIS, MINNESOTA
www.creativepub.com

Creative Publishing international

Copyright © 2012
Creative Publishing international, Inc.
400 First Avenue North, Suite 300
Minneapolis, Minnesota 55401
1-800-328-0590
www.creativepub.com

Printed in China

10 9 8 7 6 5 4 3 2 1

Library of Congress Cataloging-in-Publication Data

Advanced home wiring : current with 2012-2015 codes. -- 3rd ed.
    p. cm. -- (Complete guide)
 At head of title: Black & Decker
 Includes index.
 Summary: "This updated 3rd edition of Black & Decker's Advanced
Home Wiring features techniques, materials, and projects for
advanced home wiring installations, repairs, and maintenance,
consistent with 2012-2015 NECA codes"--Provided by publisher.
 ISBN 978-1-58923-702-5 (soft cover)
 1. Electric wiring, Interior--Amateurs' manuals. I. Creative Publish-
ing International. II. Title: Black & Decker

TK9901.A34 2012
621.319'24--dc23
                        2011052375

President/CEO: Ken Fund
Group Publisher: Bryan Trandem

Home Improvement Group

Associate Publisher: Mark Johanson
Managing Editor: Jenny Miller
Developmental Editor: Jordan Wiklund

Creative Director: Michele Lanci
Art Direction/Design: Brad Springer, Brenda Canales, Kim Winscher

Staff

Lead Photographer: Corean Komarec
Set Builder: James Parmeter
Production Managers: Laura Hokkanen, Linda Halls

Edition Editor: Chris Sibell
Page Layout Artist: Danielle Smith
Shop Help: Charles Boldt, John Keane
Technical Reviewer: Bruce Barker

Advanced Home Wiring
Created by: The Editors of Creative Publishing international, Inc., in cooperation with Black & Decker.
Black & Decker® is a trademark of The Black & Decker Corporation and is used under license.

NOTICE TO READERS

For safety, use caution, care, and good judgment when following the procedures described in this book. The publisher and Black & Decker cannot assume responsibility for any damage to property or injury to persons as a result of misuse of the information provided.

The techniques shown in this book are general techniques for various applications. In some instances, additional techniques not shown in this book may be required. Always follow manufacturers' instructions included with products, since deviating from the directions may void warranties. The projects in this book vary widely as to skill levels required: some may not be appropriate for all do-it-yourselfers, and some may require professional help.

Consult your local building department for information on building permits, codes, and other laws as they apply to your project.

Contents

Advanced Home Wiring

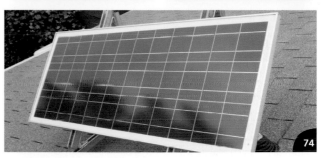

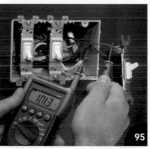
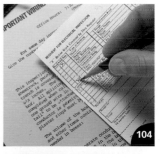

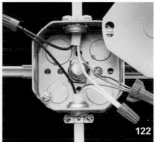

Introduction

Home wiring is a skill that is worth developing beyond the basics of replacing a switch or rewiring a lamp. There is no such thing as a simple wiring project, inasmuch as the consequences of any mistake can be severe. But advancing your skillset to include more challenging and complicated projects is the surest way to make your initial investment in the fundamentals of electrical service pay maximum dividends. This new 3rd edition of *Black & Decker Advanced Home Wiring* is directed specifically at homeowners who have some wiring experience and are interested in upgrading their capabilities.

Home wiring projects fall into three general categories: installing wiring fixtures such as ceiling lights or baseboard heaters; installing or upgrading wiring circuitry; and troubleshooting and repair. You'll find advanced-level projects in all three categories, but for the most part, the more challenging projects tend to be in the circuitry and repair groups. Almost all of the advanced wiring projects featured in this book involve new circuitry, panel upgrades, or troubleshooting with diagnostic equipment. Among the high-level projects you're not likely to find in other DIY wiring books: making a direct-current, solar-electric circuit; upgrading the grounding and bonding on your new 200-amp or larger home circuit; installing an automatic transfer switch for your backup power supply; and using a multimeter to precisely locate an open neutral in a home circuit.

Even though the projects found in this book are advanced in nature, do not attempt any of them unless you are confident in your abilities. Consult a professional electrician if you have any concerns—in many cases your best solution might be to do some of the work yourself, such as pulling new sheathed cable through walls, and to have the electrical contractor do the other work, such as making the connections. Because most wiring projects require a permit from your local building department, you will need to be able to plot out and explain clearly your project strategies, materials, and costs, and in some cases arrange for field inspections. But do keep in mind that home wiring can be a fun and fascinating pursuit, and successfully accomplishing a major project is personally gratifying and can also save you substantial amounts of money.

Working Safely

Safety should be the primary concern of anyone working with electricity. Although most household electrical repairs are simple and straightforward, always use caution and good judgment when working with electrical wiring or devices. Common sense can prevent accidents.

The basic rule of electrical safety is: Always turn off power to the area or device you are working on. At the main service panel, remove the fuse or shut off the circuit breaker that controls the circuit you are servicing. Then check to make sure the power is off by testing for power with a voltage tester. *Tip: Test a live circuit with the voltage tester to verify that it is working before you rely on it.* Restore power only when the repair or replacement project is complete.

Follow the safety tips shown on these pages. Never attempt an electrical project beyond your skill or confidence level. Never attempt to repair or replace your main service panel or service entrance head. These are jobs for a qualified electrician and require that the power company shut off power to your house.

Shut power OFF at the main service panel or the main fuse box before beginning any work.

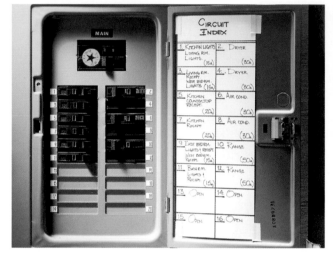

Create a circuit index and affix it to the inside of the door to your main service panel. Update it as needed.

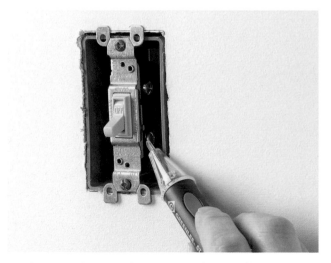

Confirm power is OFF by testing at the outlet, switch, or fixture with a voltage tester.

Use only UL-approved electrical parts or devices. These devices have been tested for safety by Underwriters Laboratories.

Tips for Working Safely

Wear rubber-soled shoes while working on electrical projects. On damp floors, stand on a rubber mat or dry wooden boards.

Use fiberglass or wood ladders when making routine household repairs near the service mast.

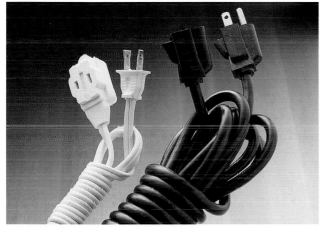

Extension cords are for temporary use only. Cords must be rated for the intended usage.

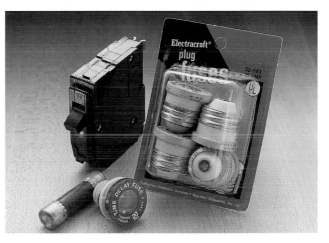

Breakers and fuses must be compatible with the panel manufacturer and match the circuit capacity.

Never alter the prongs of a plug to fit a receptacle. If possible, install a new grounded receptacle.

Do not penetrate walls or ceilings without first shutting off electrical power to the circuits that may be hidden.

(continued)

Tips for Working Safely

Anchor the cable to the side of the framing members at least 1¼" from the edge using plastic staples. NM (nonmetallic) cable should be stapled every 4½ ft. and within 8" of each electrical box.

Install metal nail guards to protect cable from damage. Nail guards are available at hardware stores and home centers.

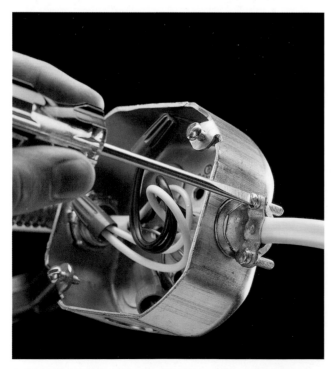

Anchor the cable to the electrical box with a cable clamp. Several types of cable clamps are available at hardware stores and home centers.

Bring installation up to code by enclosing the splice inside a metal or plastic electrical box. Make sure the box is large enough to accommodate the number of wires it contains.

Problem: Bare wire extends past a screw terminal. Exposed wire can cause a short circuit if it touches the metal box or another circuit wire.

Solution: Clip the wire and reconnect it to the screw terminal. In a proper connection, the bare wire wraps completely around the screw terminal, and the plastic insulation just touches the screw head.

Problem: A recessed electrical box is hazardous, especially if the wall or ceiling surface is made from a flammable material, like wood paneling. The National Electrical Code prohibits this type of installation.

Solution: Add an extension ring to bring the face of the electrical box flush with the surface. Extension rings come in several sizes and are available at hardware stores.

Problem: Crowded electrical box (shown cutaway) makes electrical repairs difficult. This type of installation is prohibited because wires can be damaged easily when a receptacle or switch is installed.

Solution: Replace the electrical box with a deeper electrical box.

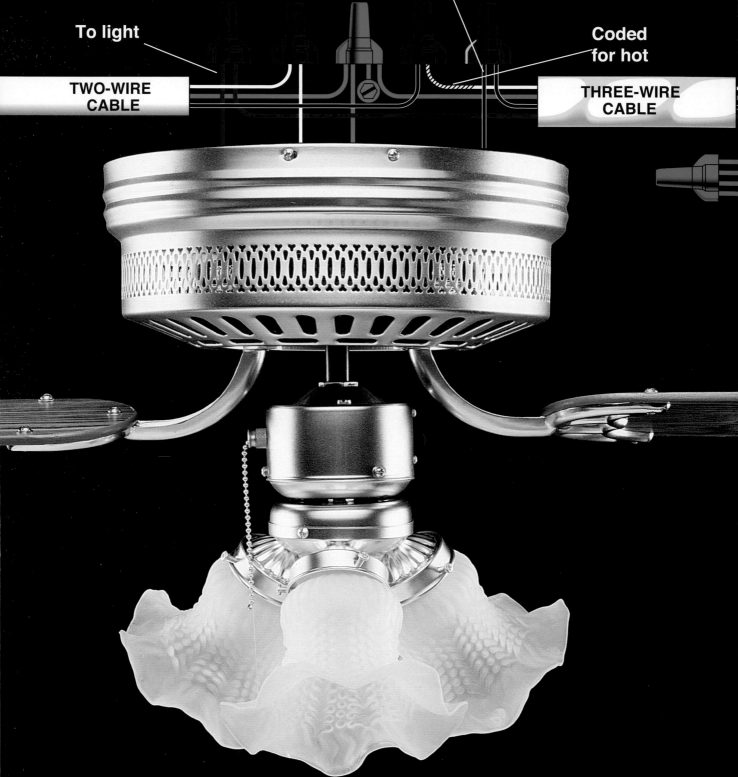

To light

Coded for hot

TWO-WIRE CABLE

THREE-WIRE CABLE

**Coded
for hot**

Circuit Maps

The circuit maps on the following pages show the most common wiring variations for typical electrical devices. Most new wiring you install will match one or more of the maps shown. Find the maps that match your situation and use them to plan your circuit layouts.

Note: For clarity, all grounding conductors in the circuit maps are colored green. In practice, the grounding wires inside sheathed cables usually are bare copper.

Circuit Maps:

1. 120-volt duplex receptacles wired in sequence

2. GFCI receptacles (single-location protection)

3. GFCI receptacle, switch & light fixture (wired for multiple location protection)

4. Single-pole switch & light fixture (light fixture at end of cable run)

5. Single-pole switch & light fixture (switch at end of cable run)

6. Single-pole switch & two light fixtures (switch between light fixtures, light at start of cable run)

7. Single-pole switch & light fixture, duplex receptacle (switch at start of cable run)

8. Switch-controlled split receptacle, duplex receptacle (switch at start of cable run)

9. Switch-controlled split receptacle (switch at end of cable run)

10. Double receptacle circuit with shared neutral wire (receptacles alternate circuits)

11. Double receptacle small-appliance circuit with GFCIs & shared neutral wire

12. Double receptacle small-appliance circuit with GFCIs & separate neutral wires

13. 120/240-volt range receptacle

14. 240-volt baseboard heaters, thermostat

15. 240-volt appliance receptacle

16. Ganged single-pole switches controlling separate light fixtures

17. Ganged switches controlling a light fixture and a vent fan

18. Three-way switches & light fixture (fixture between switches)

19. Three-way switches & light fixture (fixture at start of cable run)

20. Three-way switches & light fixture (fixture at end of cable run)

21. Three-way switches & light fixture with duplex receptacle

22. Three-way switches & multiple light fixtures (fixtures between switches)

23. Three-way switches & multiple light fixtures (fixtures at beginning of run)

24. Four-way switch & light fixture (fixture at start of cable run)

25. Four-way switch & light fixture (fixture at end of cable run)

26. Multiple four-way switches controlling a light fixture

27. Ceiling fan/light fixture controlled by ganged switches (fan at end of cable run)

28. Ceiling fan/light fixture controlled by ganged switches (switches at end of cable run)

Common Household Circuits

1. 120-VOLT DUPLEX RECEPTACLES WIRED IN SEQUENCE

Use this layout to link any number of duplex receptacles in a basic lighting/receptacle circuit. The last receptacle in the cable run is connected like the receptacle shown at the right side of the circuit map below. All other receptacles are wired like the receptacle shown on the left side. Requires two-wire cables.

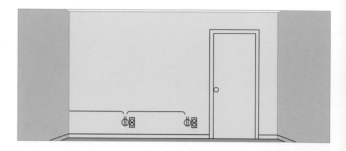

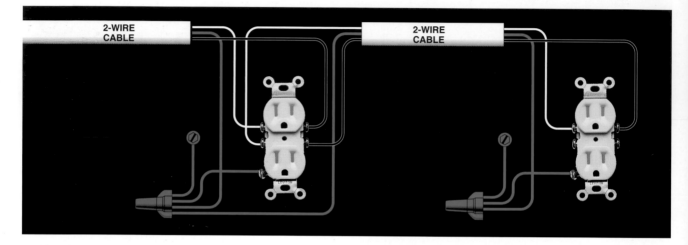

2. GFCI RECEPTACLES (SINGLE-LOCATION PROTECTION

Use this layout when receptacles located in a room with a water source, like a kitchen or a bathroom. In this configuration, only devices plugged into the GFCI receptacle will be protected—the downstream receptacle is not wired in series and will continue to function if the GFCI trips. Requires two-wire cables. Where a GFCI must protect other fixtures, use circuit map 3.

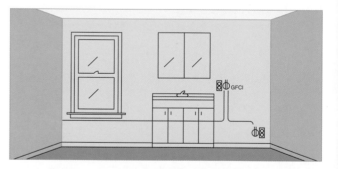

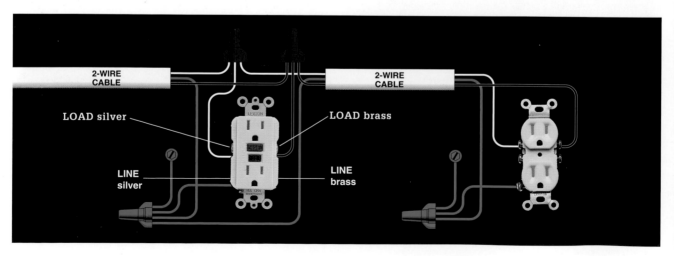

3. GFCI RECEPTACLE, SWITCH & LIGHT FIXTURE (WIRED FOR MULTIPLE-LOCATION PROTECTION)

In some locations, such as an outdoor circuit, it is a good idea to connect a GFCI receptacle so it also provides shock protection to the wires and fixtures that continue to the end of the circuit. Wires from the power source are connected to the line screw terminals; outgoing wires are connected to load screws. Requires two-wire cables.

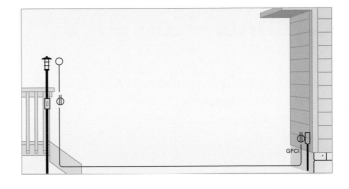

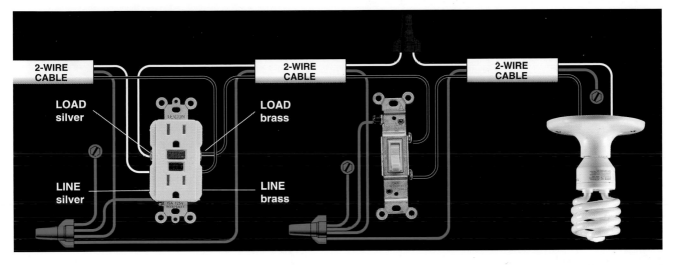

4. SINGLE-POLE SWITCH & LIGHT FIXTURE (LIGHT FIXTURE AT END OF CABLE RUN)

Use this layout for light fixtures in basic lighting/receptacle circuits throughout the home. It is often used as an extension to a series of receptacles (circuit map 1). Requires two-wire cables.

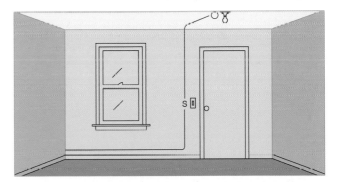

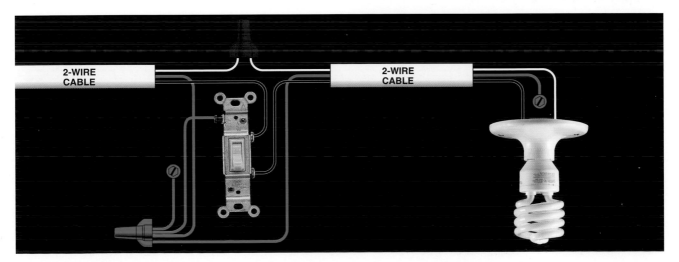

5. SINGLE-POLE SWITCH & LIGHT FIXTURE (SWITCH AT END OF CABLE RUN)

Use this layout, sometimes called a switch loop, where it is more practical to locate a switch at the end of the cable run. In the last length of cable, both insulated wires are hot; the white wire is tagged with black tape at both ends to indicate it is hot. Requires two-wire cables.

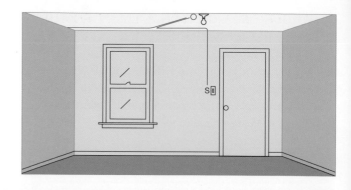

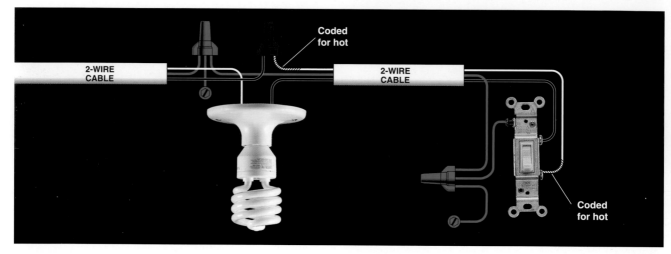

6. SINGLE-POLE SWITCH & TWO LIGHT FIXTURES (SWITCH BETWEEN LIGHT FIXTURES, LIGHT AT START OF CABLE RUN)

Use this layout when you need to control two fixtures from one single-pole switch and the switch is between the two lights in the cable run. Power feeds to one of the lights. Requires two-wire and three-wire cables.

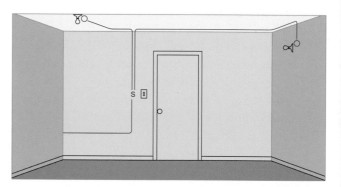

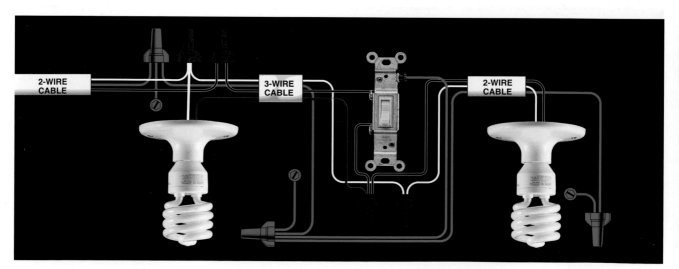

7. SINGLE-POLE SWITCH & LIGHT FIXTURE, DUPLEX RECEPTACLE (SWITCH AT START OF CABLE RUN)

Use this layout to continue a circuit past a switched light fixture to one or more duplex receptacles. To add multiple receptacles to the circuit, see circuit map 1. Requires two-wire and three-wire cables.

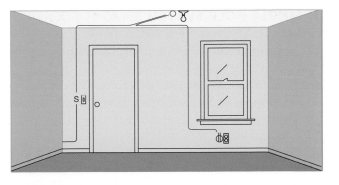

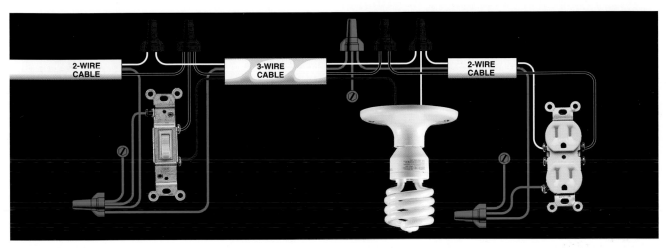

8. SWITCH-CONTROLLED SPLIT RECEPTACLE, DUPLEX RECEPTACLE (SWITCH AT START OF CABLE RUN)

This layout lets you use a wall switch to control a lamp plugged into a wall receptacle. Only the bottom half of the first receptacle is controlled by the wall switch; the top half of the receptacle and all additional receptacles on the circuit are always hot. Requires two-wire and three-wire cables.

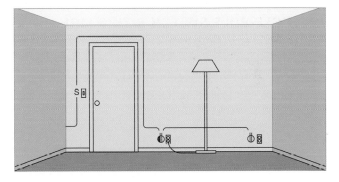

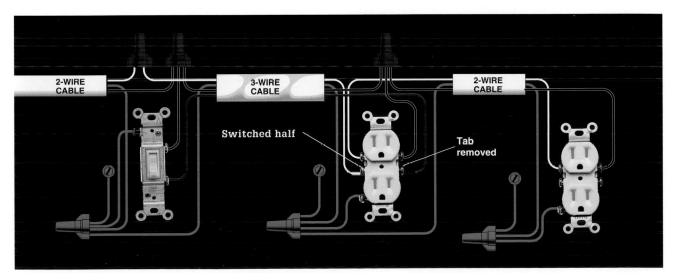

9. SWITCH-CONTROLLED SPLIT RECEPTACLE (SWITCH AT END OF CABLE RUN)

Use this switch loop layout to control a split receptacle (see circuit map 7) from an end-of-run circuit location. The bottom half of the receptacle is controlled by the wall switch, while the top half is always hot. White circuit wire attached to the switch is tagged with black tape to indicate it is hot. Requires two-wire cable.

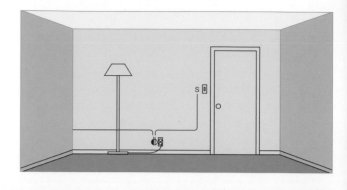

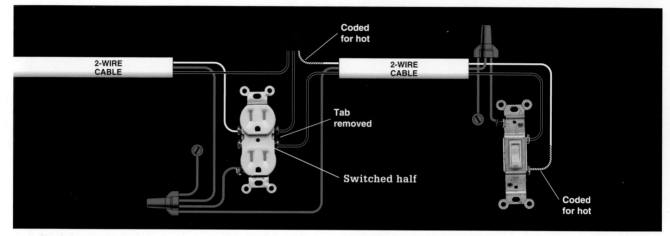

10. DOUBLE RECEPTACLE CIRCUIT WITH SHARED NEUTRAL WIRE (RECEPTACLES ALTERNATE CIRCUITS)

This layout features two 120-volt circuits wired with one three-wire cable connected to a double-pole circuit breaker. The black hot wire powers one circuit; the red wire powers the other. The white wire is a shared neutral that serves both circuits. When wired with 12/2 and 12/3 cable and GFCI receptacles rated for 20 amps, this layout can be used for the two small-appliance circuits required in a kitchen.

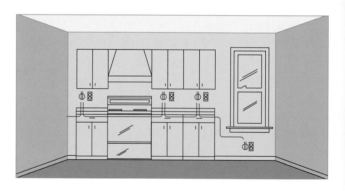

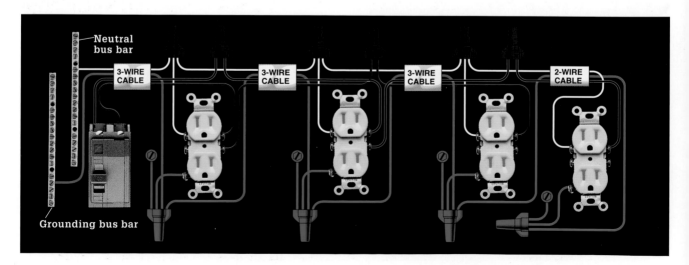

11. DOUBLE RECEPTACLE SMALL-APPLIANCE CIRCUIT WITH GFCIs & SHARED NEUTRAL WIRE

Use this layout variation of circuit map 10 to wire a double receptacle circuit when code requires that some of the receptacles be GFCIs. Each GFCI is wired for single-location protection (see circuit map 2). Requires three-wire and two-wire cables. Best used when retrofitting GFCI receptacles—in new construction it is cheaper to wire so one GFCI protects multiple locations.

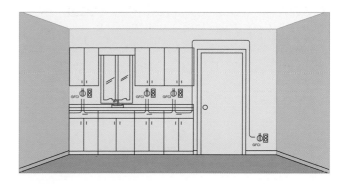

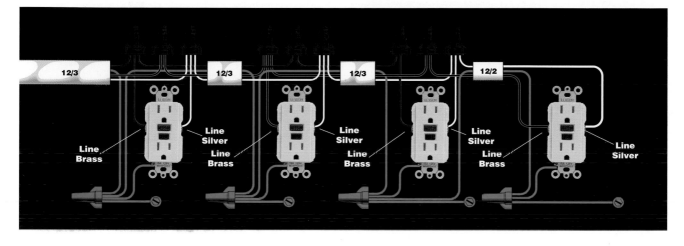

12. DOUBLE RECEPTACLE SMALL APPLIANCE CIRCUIT WITH GFCIs & SEPARATE NEUTRAL WIRES

If the room layout or local codes do not allow for a shared neutral wire, use this layout instead. The GFCIs should be wired for single location protection (see circuit map 2). Requires two-wire cable.

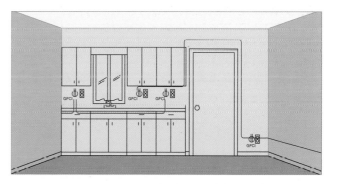

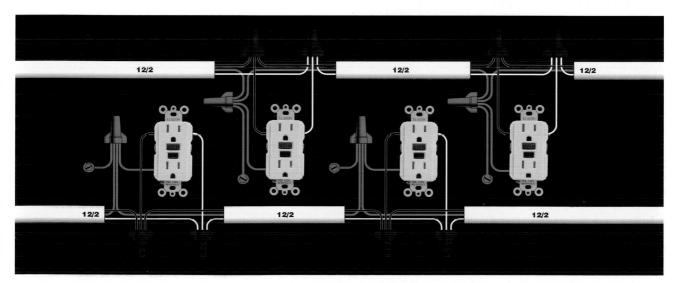

13. 120/240-VOLT RANGE RECEPTACLE

This layout is for a 40- or 50-amp, 120/240-volt dedicated appliance circuit wired with 8/3 or 6/3 copper cable, as required by code for a large kitchen range. The black and red circuit wires, connected to a double-pole circuit breaker in the circuit breaker panel, each bring 120 volts of power to the setscrew terminals on the receptacle. The white circuit wire attached to the neutral bus bar in the circuit breaker panel is connected to the neutral setscrew terminal on the receptacle.

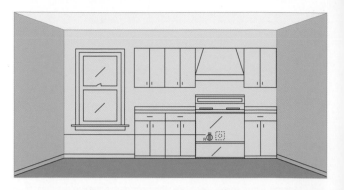

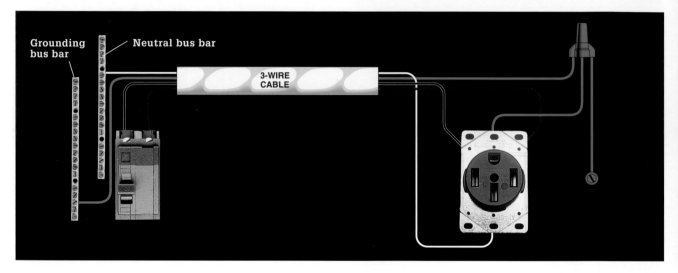

14. 240-VOLT BASEBOARD HEATERS, THERMOSTAT

This layout is typical for a series of 240-volt baseboard heaters controlled by a wall thermostat. Except for the last heater in the circuit, all heaters are wired as shown below. The last heater is connected to only one cable. The size of the circuit and cables are determined by finding the total wattage of all heaters. Requires two-wire cable.

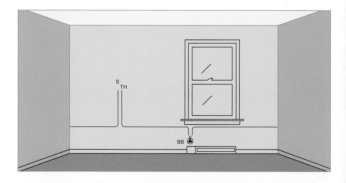

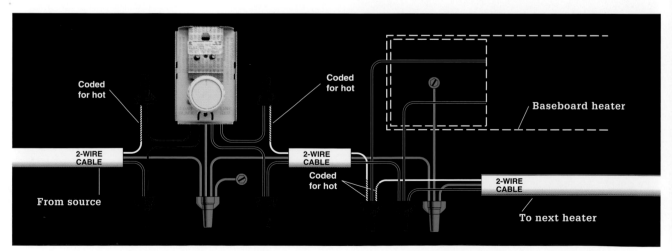

15. 240-VOLT APPLIANCE RECEPTACLE

This layout represents a 20-amp, 240-volt dedicated appliance circuit wired with 12/2 cable, as required by code for a large window air conditioner. Receptacles are available in both singleplex (shown) and duplex styles. The black and the white circuit wires connected to a double-pole breaker each bring 120 volts of power to the receptacle (combined, they bring 240 volts). The white wire is tagged with black tape to indicate it is hot.

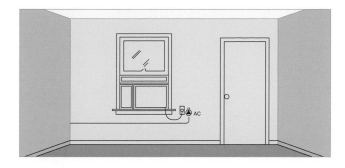

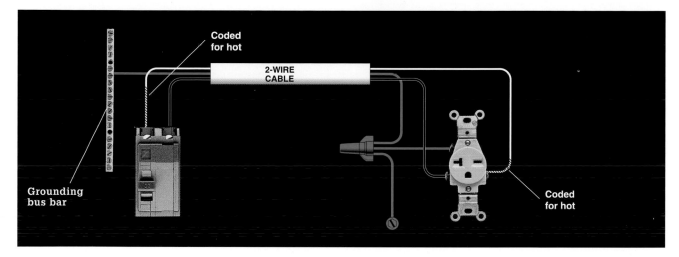

16. GANGED SINGLE-POLE SWITCHES CONTROLLING SEPARATE LIGHT FIXTURES

This layout lets you place two switches controlled by the same 120-volt circuit in one double-gang electrical box. A single feed cable provides power to both switches. A similar layout with two feed cables can be used to place switches from different circuits in the same box. Requires two-wire cable.

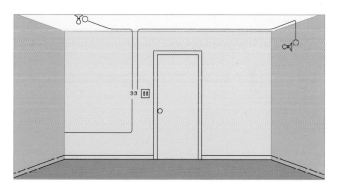

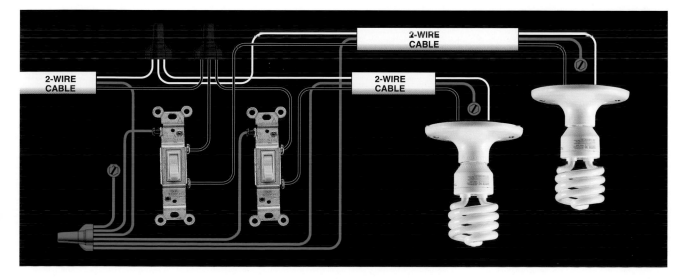

17. GANGED SWITCHES CONTROLLING A LIGHT FIXTURE AND A VENT FAN

This layout lets you place two switches controlled by the same 120-volt circuit in one double-gang electrical box. A single feed cable provides power to both switches. A standard switch controls the light fixture and a time-delay switch controls the vent fan.

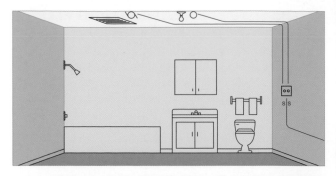

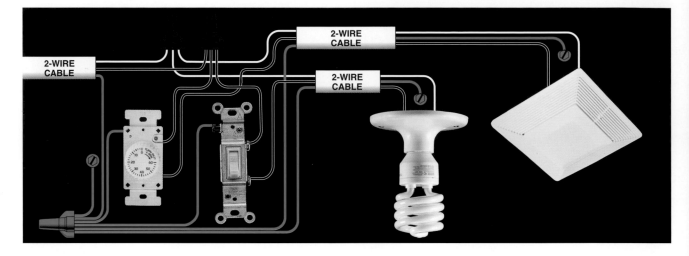

18. THREE-WAY SWITCHES & LIGHT FIXTURE (FIXTURE BETWEEN SWITCHES)

This layout for three-way switches lets you control a light fixture from two locations. Each switch has one common screw terminal and two traveler screws. Circuit wires attached to the traveler screws run between the two switches, and hot wires attached to the common screws bring current from the power source and carry it to the light fixture. Requires two-wire and three-wire cables.

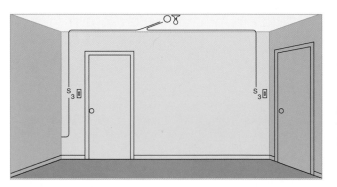

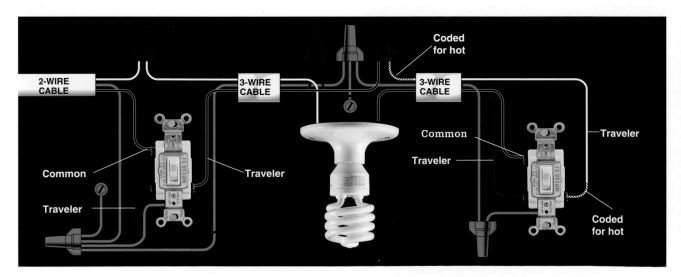

19. THREE-WAY SWITCHES & LIGHT FIXTURE (FIXTURE AT START OF CABLE RUN)

Use this layout variation of circuit map 19 where it is more convenient to locate the fixture ahead of the three-way switches in the cable run. Requires two-wire and three-wire cables.

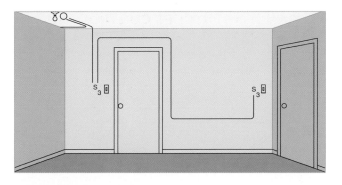

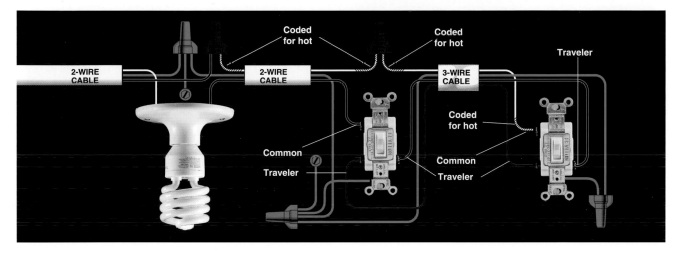

20. THREE-WAY SWITCHES & LIGHT FIXTURE (FIXTURE AT END OF CABLE RUN)

This variation of the three-way switch layout (circuit map 20) is used where it is more practical to locate the fixture at the end of the cable run. Requires two-wire and three-wire cables.

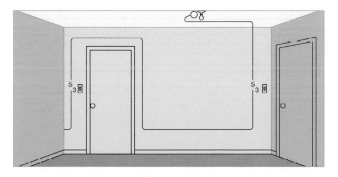

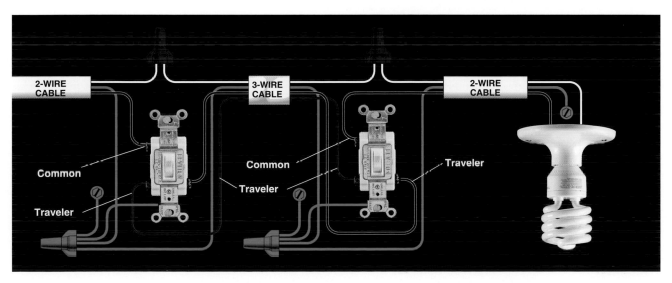

21. THREE-WAY SWITCHES & LIGHT FIXTURE WITH DUPLEX RECEPTACLE

Use this layout to add a receptacle to a three-way switch configuration (circuit map 21). Requires two-wire and three-wire cables.

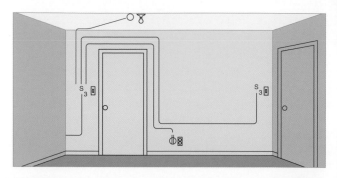

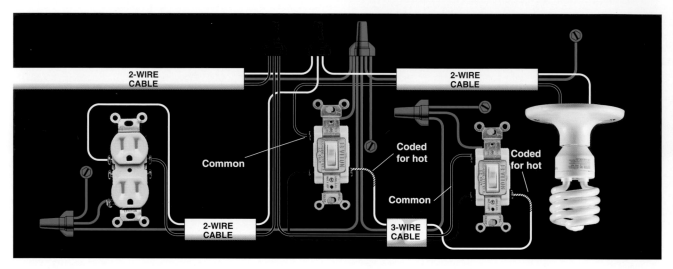

22. THREE-WAY SWITCHES & MULTIPLE LIGHT FIXTURES (FIXTURES BETWEEN SWITCHES)

This is a variation of circuit map 20. Use it to place multiple light fixtures between two three-way switches where power comes in at one of the switches. Requires two- and three-wire cable.

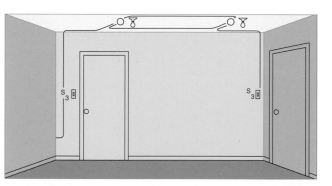

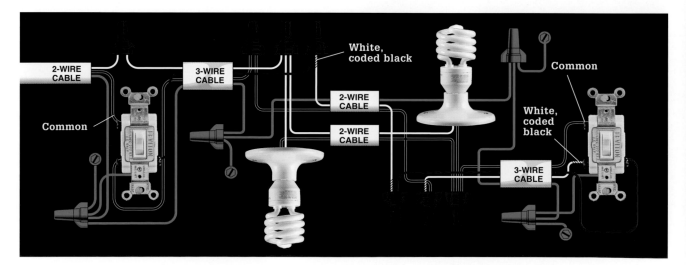

23. THREE-WAY SWITCHES & MULTIPLE LIGHT FIXTURES (FIXTURES AT BEGINNING OF RUN)

This is a variation of circuit map 21. Use it to place multiple light fixtures at the beginning of a run controlled by two three-way switches. Power comes in at the first fixture. Requires two- and three-wire cable.

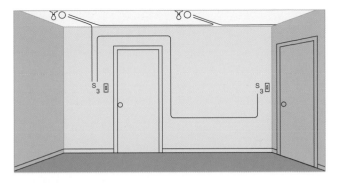

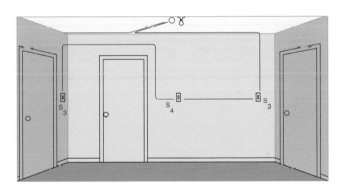

24. FOUR-WAY SWITCH & LIGHT FIXTURE (FIXTURE AT START OF CABLE RUN)

This layout lets you control a light fixture from three locations. The end switches are three-way and the middle is four-way. A pair of three-wire cables enter the box of the four-way switch. The white and red wires from one cable attach to the top pair of screw terminals (line 1) and the white and red wires from the other cable attaches to the bottom screw terminals (line 2). Requires two three-way switches and one four-way switch and two-wire and three-wire cables.

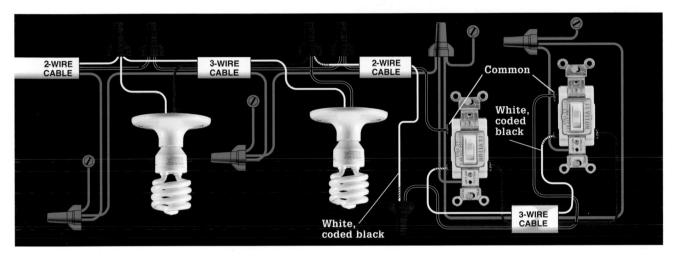

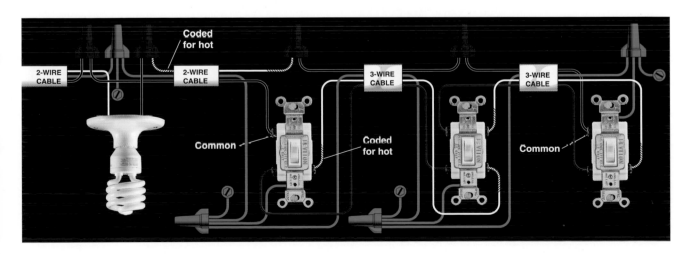

25. FOUR-WAY SWITCH & LIGHT FIXTURE (FIXTURE AT END OF CABLE RUN)

Use this layout variation of circuit map 26 where it is more practical to locate the fixture at the end of the cable run. Requires two three-way switches and one four-way switch and two-wire and three-wire cables.

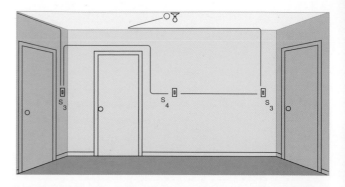

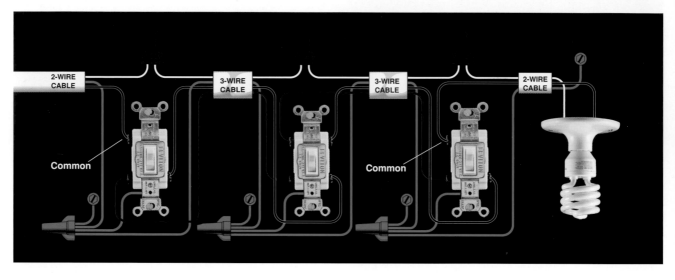

26. MULTIPLE FOUR-WAY SWITCHES CONTROLLING A LIGHT FIXTURE

This alternate variation of the four-way switch layout (circuit map 27) is used where three or more switches will control a single fixture. The outer switches are three-way and the middle are four-way. Requires two three-way switches and two four-way switches and two-wire and three-wire cables.

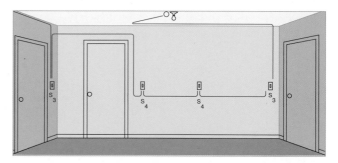

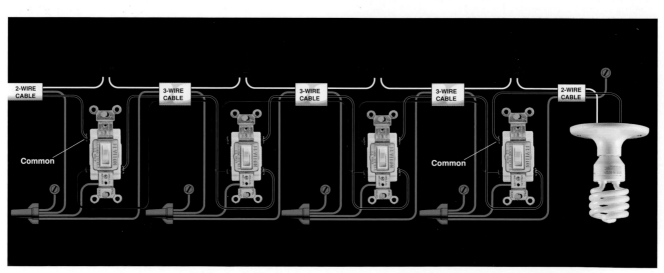

27. CEILING FAN/LIGHT FIXTURE CONTROLLED BY GANGED SWITCHES (FAN AT END OF CABLE RUN)

This layout is for a combination ceiling fan/light fixture controlled by a speed-control switch and dimmer in a double-gang switch box. Requires two-wire and three-wire cables.

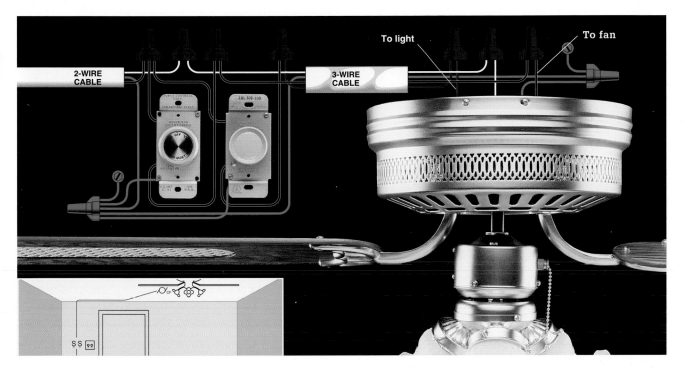

28. CEILING FAN/LIGHT FIXTURE CONTROLLED BY GANGED SWITCHES (SWITCHES AT END OF CABLE RUN)

Use this switch loop layout variation when it is more practical to install the ganged speed control and dimmer switches for the ceiling fan at the end of the cable run. Requires two-wire and three-wire cables.

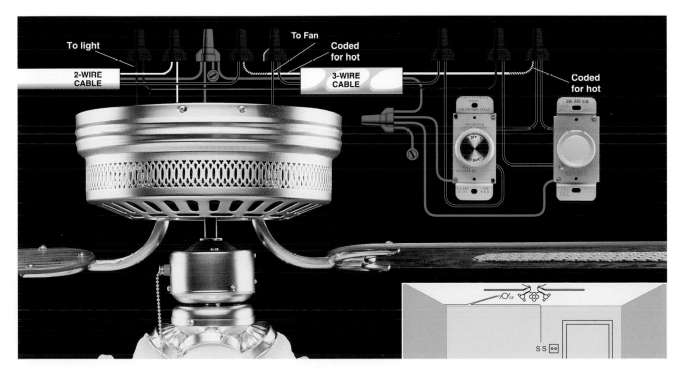

Advanced Wiring Projects

The following pages contain step-by-step information and photos that reveal exactly how to accomplish several of the most common advanced home wiring projects. Most of these projects fall into three basic categories: panel projects that are accomplished in the main service panel or an electrical subpanel; adding new electrical circuits; and troubleshooting. To allow ample space for demonstrating the specific techniques and strategies that are necessary for these projects, we have not gone into great detail for some of the more basic planning and materials-handling steps that every project should include—no matter how advanced it may be. Basic mapping of your system and circuitry, estimating materials, applying for permits and arranging for inspections are all important to the safe conduct of any electrical project. If you are unfamiliar with the requirements for any of these steps, consult your local electrical inspector for advice. Drawing an accurate circuit map may not be glamorous or "advanced" in some definitions, but it is critically important.

In this chapter:

- Electrical Panels
- Installing Circuit Breakers
- Installing a Subpanel
- Upgrading Service Panels
- Grounding & Bonding an Upgraded System
- Adding Circuits
- Wiring a Room Addition
- Wiring a Kitchen
- Installing a Solar Light Circuit
- Backup Power Supply

- Installing a Transfer Switch
- Common Residential Wiring Codes
- Electrical Receptacle Installation
- Ground-fault (GFCI) & Arc-fault (AFCI) Protection
- Junction Boxes, Device Boxes & Enclosures

Electrical Panels

Every home has a main service panel that distributes electrical current to the individual circuits. The main service panel usually is found in the basement, garage, or utility area, and can be identified by its metal casing. Before making any repair to your electrical system, you must shut off power to the correct circuit at the main service panel. The service panel should be indexed so circuits can be identified easily.

Service panels vary in appearance, depending on the age of the system. Very old wiring may operate on 30-amp service that has only two circuits. New homes can have 200-amp service with 30 or more circuits. Find the size of the service by reading the amperage rating printed on the main fuse block or main circuit breaker.

Regardless of age, all service panels have fuses or circuit breakers that control each circuit and protect them from overloads. In general, older service panels use fuses, while newer service panels use circuit breakers.

In addition to the main service panel, your electrical system may have a subpanel that controls some of the circuits in the home. A subpanel has its own circuit breakers or fuses and is installed to control circuits that have been added to an existing wiring system.

The subpanel resembles the main service panel but is usually smaller. It may be located near the main panel, or it may be found near the areas served by the new circuits. Garages and basements that have been updated often have their own subpanels. If your home has a subpanel, make sure that its circuits are indexed correctly.

When handling fuses or circuit breakers, make sure the area around the service panel is dry. Never remove the protective cover on the service panel. After turning off a circuit to make electrical repairs, remember to always test the circuit for power before touching any wires.

The main service panel is the heart of your wiring system. As our demand for household energy has increased, the panels have also grown in capacity. Today, a 200-amp panel is considered the minimum for new construction.

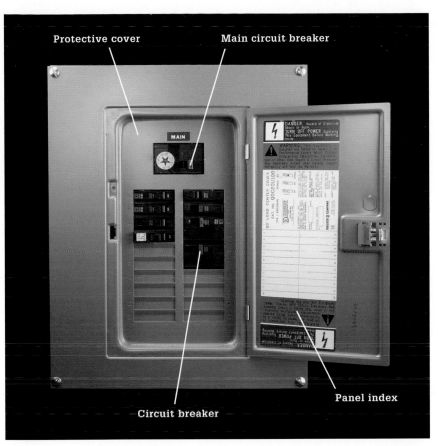

Protective cover   Main circuit breaker

MAIN

DANGER Hazard of Electrical Shock or Burn. TURN OFF POWER Supplying This Equipment Before Working Inside.

Panel index

Circuit breaker

A circuit breaker panel providing 100 amps or more of power is common in wiring systems installed during the 1960s and later. A circuit breaker panel is housed in a gray metal cabinet that contains two rows of individual circuit breakers. The size of the service can be identified by reading the amperage rating of the main circuit breaker, which is located at the top or bottom of the main service panel.

A 100-amp service panel is now the minimum standard for all new housing. It is considered adequate for a medium-sized house with no more than three major electric appliances. However, most newer houses have a 200-amp or larger panel.

To shut off power to individual circuits in a circuit breaker panel, flip the lever on the appropriate circuit breaker to the OFF position. To shut off the power to the entire house, turn the main circuit breaker or breakers to the OFF position.

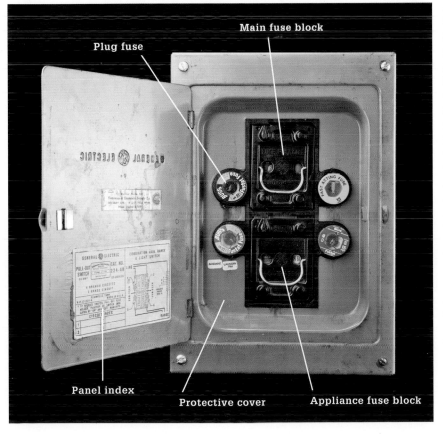

Plug fuse   Main fuse block

GENERAL ELECTRIC

Panel index

Protective cover   Appliance fuse block

A 60-amp fuse panel often is found in wiring systems installed between 1950 and 1965. It usually is housed in a gray metal cabinet that contains four individual plug fuses, plus one or two pull-out fuse blocks that hold cartridge fuses. This type of panel is regarded as adequate for a small, 1,100-square-foot house that has no more than one 240-volt appliance. Many homeowners update 60-amp service to 100 amps or more so that additional lighting and appliance circuits can be added to the system. Home loan programs also may require that 60-amp service be updated before a home can qualify for financing.

To shut off power to a circuit, carefully unscrew the plug fuse, touching only its insulated rim. To shut off power to the entire house, hold the handle of the main fuse block and pull sharply to remove it. Major appliance circuits are controlled with another cartridge fuse block. Shut off the appliance circuit by pulling out this fuse block.

Circuit Breaker Panels

The circuit breaker panel is the electrical distribution center for your home. It divides the current into branch circuits that are carried throughout the house. Each branch circuit is controlled by a circuit breaker that protects the wires from dangerous current overloads. When installing new circuits, the last step is to connect the wires to new circuit breakers at the panel. Working inside a circuit breaker panel is not dangerous if you follow basic safety procedures. Always shut off the main circuit breaker and test for power before touching any parts inside the panel, and never touch the service wire lugs. If unsure of your own skills, hire an electrician to make the final circuit connections. (If you have an older electrical service with fuses instead of circuit breakers, always have an electrician make these final hookups.)

If the main circuit breaker panel does not have enough open slots to hold new circuit breakers, install a subpanel (page 34). This job is well within the skill level of an experienced do-it-yourselfer,

Slimline circuit breakers require half as much space as standard single-pole breakers. Slimlines can be used to make room for added circuits.

Grounding bus bar has terminals for linking grounding wires to the main grounding conductor. It is bonded to the neutral bus bar.

Main circuit breaker panel distributes the power entering the home into branch circuits.

Neutral service wire carries current back to the power source after it has passed through the home.

Two hot service wires provide 120/240 volts of power to the main circuit breaker. These wires are always HOT.

Main circuit breaker protects the hot service wires from overloads and transfers power to two hot bus bars.

Double-pole breaker wired for a 120/240 circuit transfers power from the two hot bus bars to red and black hot wires in a three-wire cable.

Neutral bus bar has setscrew terminals for linking all neutral circuit wires to the neutral service wire.

Service wire lugs: DO NOT TOUCH

120-volt branch circuits

Subpanel feeder breaker is a double-pole breaker, usually 30 to 50 amps. It is wired in the same way as a 120/240-volt circuit.

Two hot bus bars run through the center of the panel, supplying power to the circuit breakers. Each carries 120 volts.

Grounding conductor leads to metal grounding rods driven into the earth.

120/240-volt branch circuit

although you can also hire an electrician to install the subpanel.

Before installing any new wiring, evaluate your electrical service to make sure it provides enough current to support both the existing wiring and any new circuits. If your service does not provide enough power, have an electrician upgrade it to a higher amp rating. During the upgrade, the electrician will install a new circuit breaker panel with enough extra breaker slots for the new circuits you want to install.

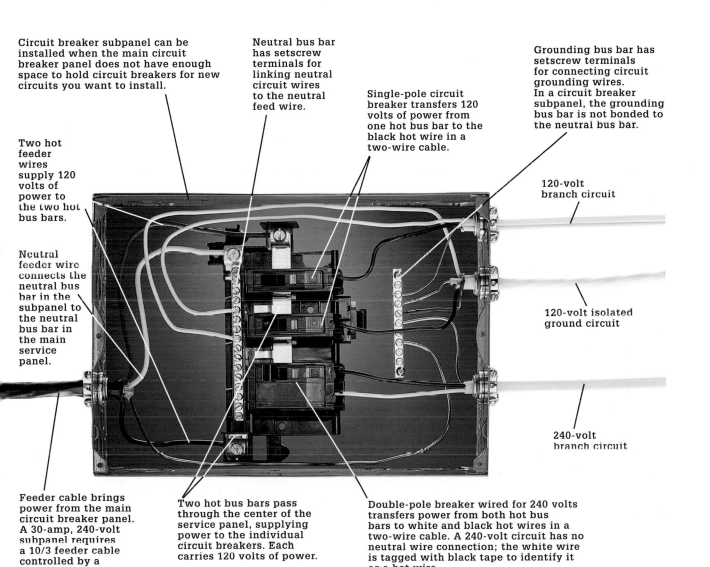

Circuit breaker subpanel can be installed when the main circuit breaker panel does not have enough space to hold circuit breakers for new circuits you want to install.

Neutral bus bar has setscrew terminals for linking neutral circuit wires to the neutral feed wire.

Single-pole circuit breaker transfers 120 volts of power from one hot bus bar to the black hot wire in a two-wire cable.

Grounding bus bar has setscrew terminals for connecting circuit grounding wires. In a circuit breaker subpanel, the grounding bus bar is not bonded to the neutral bus bar.

Two hot feeder wires supply 120 volts of power to the two hot bus bars.

120-volt branch circuit

Neutral feeder wire connects the neutral bus bar in the subpanel to the neutral bus bar in the main service panel.

120-volt isolated ground circuit

240-volt branch circuit

Feeder cable brings power from the main circuit breaker panel. A 30-amp, 240-volt subpanel requires a 10/3 feeder cable controlled by a 30-amp double-pole circuit breaker.

Two hot bus bars pass through the center of the service panel, supplying power to the individual circuit breakers. Each carries 120 volts of power.

Double-pole breaker wired for 240 volts transfers power from both hot bus bars to white and black hot wires in a two-wire cable. A 240-volt circuit has no neutral wire connection; the white wire is tagged with black tape to identify it as a hot wire.

Installing Circuit Breakers

The last step in a wiring project is connecting circuits at the breaker panel. After this is done, the work is ready for the final inspection.

Circuits are connected at the main breaker panel, if it has enough open slots, or at a circuit breaker subpanel (page 34). When working at a subpanel, make sure the feeder breaker at the main panel has been turned off, and test for power (photo, right) before touching any parts in the subpanel.

Make sure the circuit breaker amperage does not exceed the ampacity of the circuit wires you are connecting to it. Also be aware that circuit breaker styles and installation techniques vary according to manufacturer. Use breakers designed for your type of panel. For most rooms in a home, in addition to the kitchen, basement, and bathroom, an AFCI breaker needs to be installed.

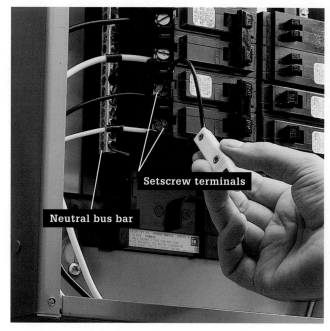

Setscrew terminals

Neutral bus bar

Test for current before touching any parts inside a circuit breaker panel. With main breaker turned off but all other breakers turned on, touch one probe of a neon tester to the neutral bus bar, and touch the other probe to each setscrew on one of the double-pole breakers (not the main breaker). If tester does not light for either setscrew, it is safe to work in the panel. *Note: Touchless circuit testers are preferred in most situations where you are testing for current because they're safer. But in some instances you'll need a tester with individual probes to properly check for current.*

Tools & Materials ▸

Screwdriver	Circuit tester
Hammer	Pliers
Pencil	Cable clamps
Combination tool	Single- and double-pole
Cable ripper	circuit breakers

How to Connect Circuit Breakers

1

Shut off the main circuit breaker in the main circuit breaker panel (if you are working in a subpanel, shut off the feeder breaker in the main panel). Remove the panel cover plate, taking care not to touch the parts inside the panel. Test for power (photo, top).

2

Open a knockout in the side of the circuit breaker panel using a screwdriver and hammer. Attach a cable clamp to the knockout.

3

Hold cable across the front of the panel near the knockout, and mark sheathing about ½" inside the edge of the panel. Strip the cable from the marked line to the end using a cable ripper. (There should be 18" to 24" of excess cable.) Insert the cable through the clamp and into the service panel, then tighten the clamp.

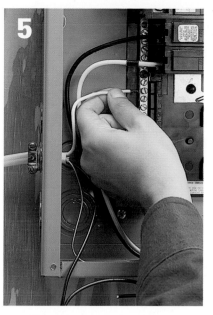

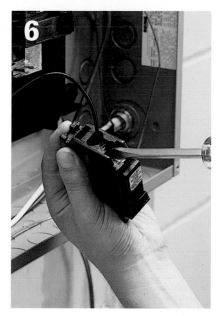

Bend the bare copper grounding wire around the inside edge of the panel to an open setscrew terminal on the grounding bus bar. Insert the wire into the opening on the bus bar, and tighten the setscrew. Fold excess wire around the inside edge of the panel.

For 120-volt circuits, bend the white circuit wire around the outside of the panel to an open setscrew terminal on the neutral bus bar. Clip away excess wire, then strip ½" of insulation from the wire using a combination tool. Insert the wire into the terminal opening, and tighten the setscrew.

Strip ½" of insulation from the end of the black circuit wire. Insert the wire into the setscrew terminal on a new single-pole circuit breaker, and tighten the setscrew.

Slide one end of the circuit breaker onto the guide hook, then press it firmly against the bus bar until it snaps into place. (Breaker installation may vary, depending on the manufacturer.) Fold excess black wire around the inside edge of the panel.

Variations: 120/240-volt circuits (top): Connect red and black wires to double-pole breaker. Connect white wire to neutral bus bar, and grounding wire to grounding bus bar. For 240-volt circuits (bottom), attach white and black wires to double-pole breaker, tagging white wire with black tape. There is no neutral bus bar connection on this circuit.

Tip: Remove the appropriate breaker knockout on the panel cover plate to make room for the new circuit breaker. A single-pole breaker requires one knockout, while a double-pole breaker requires two knockouts. Reattach the cover plate, and label the new circuit on the panel index.

Installing a Subpanel

Install a circuit breaker subpanel if the main circuit breaker panel does not have enough open breaker slots for the new circuits you are planning. Called non-service rated panels in most code books, the subpanel serves as a second distribution center for connecting circuits. It receives power from a double-pole feeder circuit breaker you install in the main circuit breaker panel.

If the main service panel is so full that there is no room for the double-pole subpanel feeder breaker, you can reconnect some of the existing 120-volt circuits to special slimline breakers (photos below). *Note: There are limits to how many slimline breakers you may use in a single panel.*

Plan your subpanel installation carefully, making sure your electrical service supplies enough power to support the extra load of the new subpanel circuits. Assuming your main service is adequate, consider installing an oversized subpanel feeder breaker in the main panel to provide enough extra amps to meet the needs of future wiring projects.

Also consider the physical size of the subpanel, and choose one that has enough extra slots to hold circuits you may want to install later. The smallest

panels have room for up to six single-pole breakers (or three double-pole breakers), while the largest models can hold up to 20 single-pole breakers.

Subpanels often are mounted near the main circuit breaker panel. Or, for convenience, they can be installed close to the areas they serve, such as in a new room addition or a garage. In a finished room, a subpanel can be painted or housed in a decorative cabinet so it is less of a visual distraction. If it is covered, make sure the subpanel is easily accessible and clearly identified.

Tools & Materials ▶

Hammer	Cable clamps
Screwdriver	Three-wire NM cable
Circuit tester	Cable staples
Cable ripper	Double-pole circuit breaker
Combination tool	Circuit breaker subpanel
Screws	Slimline circuit breakers

To conserve space in a service panel, you can replace single-pole breakers with slimline breakers. Slimline breakers take up half the space of standard breakers, allowing you to fit two circuits into one single slot on the service panel. In the service panel shown above, four single-pole 120-volt breakers were replaced with slimline breakers to provide the double opening needed for a 30-amp, 240-volt subpanel feeder breaker. Use slimline breakers (if your municipality allows them) with the same amp rating as the standard single-pole breakers you are removing, and make sure they are approved for use in your panel.

How to Install a Subpanel

Mount the subpanel at shoulder height following manufacturer's recommendations. The subpanel can be mounted to the sides of studs or to plywood attached between two studs. Panel shown here extends ½" past the face of studs so it will be flush with the finished wall surface.

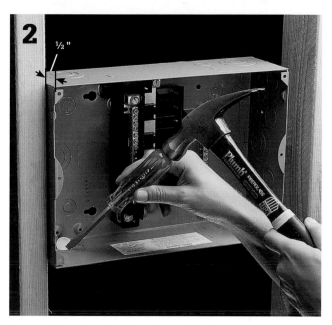

Open a knockout in the subpanel using a screwdriver and hammer. Run the feeder cable from the main circuit breaker panel to the subpanel, leaving about 2 ft. of excess cable at each end.

Attach a cable clamp to the knockout in the subpanel. Insert the cable into the subpanel, then anchor it to framing members within 8" of each panel, and every 4 ft. thereafter.

Tips for a Subpanel Installation ▸

1. Calculate your maximum feeder load (consult your local electrical inspector) and multiply by 1.25. This safety adjustment is required by the National Electrical Code. Convert the load into amps by dividing by 230. This gives the required amperage needed to power the subpanel.

2. For the subpanel feeder breaker, choose a double-pole circuit breaker with an amp rating equal to or greater than the required subpanel amperage. Example: In a room addition that requires 27 amps, choose a 30-amp double-pole feeder breaker.

3. For the feeder cable bringing power from the main circuit breaker panel to the subpanel, choose three-wire NM copper cable with an ampacity equal to the rating of the subpanel feeder breaker. Example: For a 40-amp subpanel feeder breaker, choose 8/3 cable for the feeder.

4. If the subpanel is installed in a separate building from the primary dwelling, such as a garage, the subpanel must be grounded to earth with its own ground rod.

(continued)

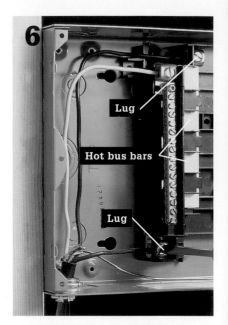

Strip away outer sheathing from the feeder cable using a cable ripper. Leave at least ¼" of sheathing extending into the subpanel. Tighten the cable clamp screws so cable is held securely but not so tightly that the wire sheathing is crushed.

Strip ½" of insulation from the white neutral feeder wire, and attach it to the main lug on the subpanel neutral bus bar. Connect the grounding wire to a setscrew terminal on the grounding bus bar. Fold excess wire around the inside edge of the subpanel.

Strip away ½" of insulation from the red and the black feeder wires. Attach one wire to the main lug on each of the hot bus bars. Fold excess wire around the inside edge of the subpanel.

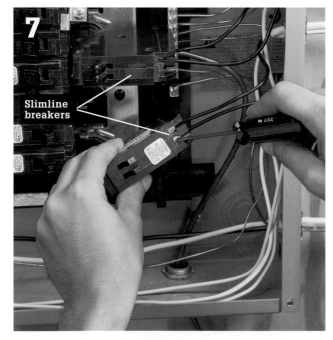

At the main circuit breaker panel, shut off the main circuit breaker, then remove the coverplate and test for power (page 32). If necessary, make room for the double-pole feeder breaker by removing single-pole breakers and reconnecting the wires to slimline circuit breakers. Open a knockout for the feeder cable using a hammer and screwdriver.

Strip away the outer sheathing from the feeder cable so that at least ¼" of sheathing will reach into the main service panel. Attach a cable clamp to the cable, then insert the cable into the knockout, and anchor it by threading a locknut onto the clamp. Tighten the locknut by driving a screwdriver against the lugs. Tighten the clamp screws so the cable is held securely, but not so tightly that the cable sheathing is crushed.

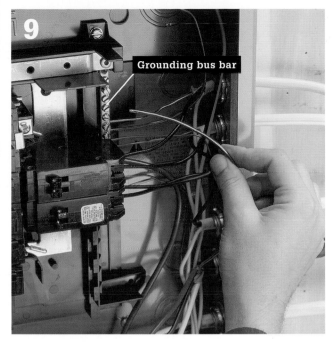

Bend the bare copper wire from the feeder cable around the inside edge of the main circuit breaker panel, and connect it to one of the setscrew terminals on the grounding bus bar.

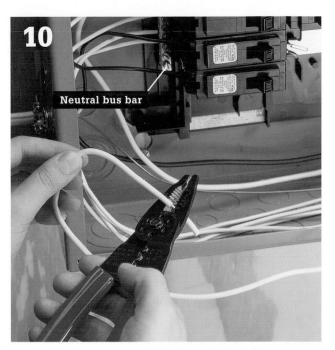

Strip away ½" of insulation from the white feeder wire. Attach the wire to one of the setscrew terminals on the neutral bus bar. Fold excess wire around the inside edge of the service panel.

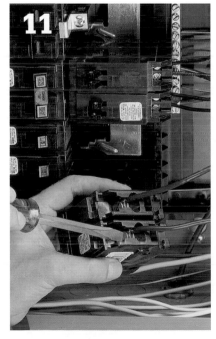

Strip ½" of insulation from the red and the black feeder wires. Attach one wire to each of the setscrew terminals on the double-pole feeder breaker. *Note: If your subpanel arrived with a preinstalled grounding screw in the panel back, remove and discard it.*

Hook the end of the feeder circuit breaker over the guide hooks on the panel, then push the other end forward until the breaker snaps onto the hot bus bars (follow manufacturer's directions). Fold excess wire around the inside edge of the circuit breaker panel.

If necessary, open two knockouts where the double-pole feeder breaker will fit, then reattach the cover plate. Label the feeder breaker on the circuit index. Turn main breaker on, but leave feeder breaker off until all subpanel circuits have been connected and inspected.

Upgrading Service Panels

Only a generation ago, fuse boxes were commonplace. But as our demands for power increased, homeowners replaced the 60-amp boxes with larger, safer, and more reliable circuit breaker panels. Typical new homes were built with perfectly adequate 100-amp load centers. But today, as average home size has risen to more than 2,500 sq. ft. and the number of home electronics has risen exponentially, 100 amps is adequate service. As a result, many homeowners have upgraded to 200-amp service, and new single-family homes often include 250 amps or even 400 amps of power.

Upgrading your electrical service panel from 100 amps to 200 amps is an ambitious project that requires a lot of forethought. To do the job, you will need to have your utility company disconnect your house from electrical service at the transformer that feeds your house. Not only does this involve working them into your schedule, it means you will have no power during the project. You can rent a portable generator to provide a circuit or two, or you can run a couple extension cords from a friendly neighbor. But unless you are a very fast worker, plan on being without power for at least one to two days while the project is in process.

Also check with your utility company to make sure you know what equipment is theirs and what belongs to you. In most cases, the electric meter and everything on the street side belongs to the power company, and the meter base and everything on the house side is yours. Be aware that if you tamper with the sealed meter in any way, you likely will be fined. Utility companies will not re-energize your system without approval from your inspecting agency.

Upgrading a service panel is a major project. Do not hesitate to call for help at any point if you're unsure what to do. It is a good idea to alert your utility about the upgrades. They can check the service drop size to make sure it is adequate.

Tools & Materials ▸

200-amp load center (service panel)	Service entry cable
	Circuit wires
200-amp bypass meter base	Plywood backer board
	Screwdrivers
Circuit breakers	Drill/driver
Schedule 80 or IMC conduit and fittings	Tape
	Allen wrench
	Circuit tester
Weatherhead	Multimeter

After: 200 amps

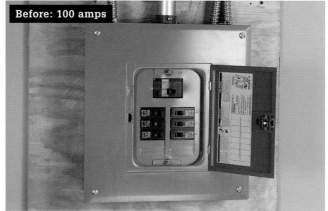

Before: 100 amps

Modern homeowners consume more power than our forebears, and it is often necessary to upgrade the electrical service to keep pace. While homeowners are not allowed to make the final electrical service connections, removing the old panel and installing the new panel and meter base yourself can save you hundreds or even thousands of dollars.

Service Entry Options

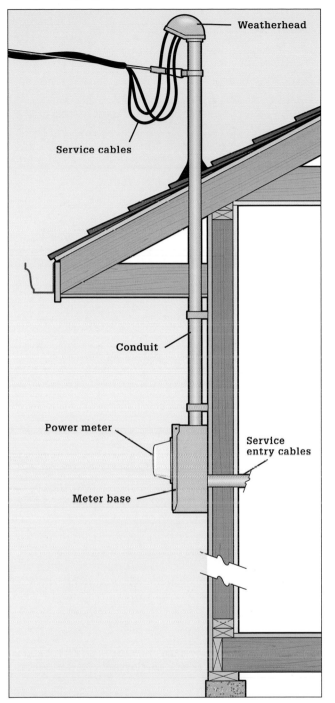

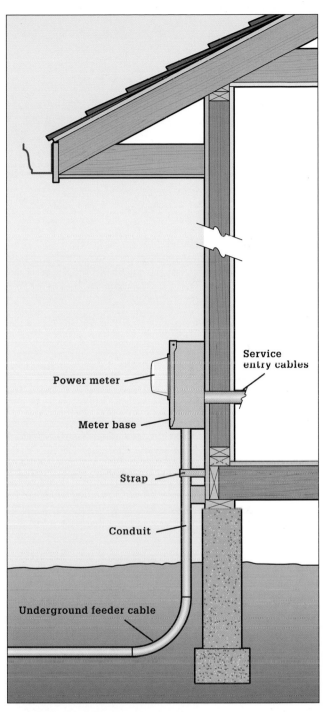

Aboveground meter with riser. In this common configuration, the power cables from the closest transformer (called the service drop) are connected to the power distribution system in your house inside a protective hood called a weatherhead. The service cables from the weatherhead are routed to a power meter that's owned by your utility company but is housed in a base that's considered your property. From the meter the cables (called service entry conductors or SECs) enter your house through the wall and are routed to the main service panel, where they are connected to the main circuit breaker.

Underground service lateral. Increasingly, homebuilders are choosing to have power supplied to their new homes underground instead of an overhead service drop. Running the cables in the ground eliminates problems with power outages caused by ice accumulation or fallen trees, but it entails a completely different set of cable and conduit requirements. For the homeowner, however, the differences are minimal because the hookups are identical once the power service reaches the meter.

Locating Your New Panel ▸

Local codes dictate where the main service panel may be placed relative to other parts of your home. Although the codes may vary (and always take precedence), national codes stipulate that a service panel (or any other distribution panel) may not be located near flammable materials, in a bathroom, or directly above a workbench or other permanent work station or appliance. The panel also can't be located in a crawl space. The panel must be framed with at least 36" of clear space on all sides. If you are installing a new service entry hookup, there are many regulations regarding height of the service drop and the meter (the meter should be located 66" above grade). Contact your local inspections office for specific regulations.

All the equipment you'll need to upgrade your main panel is sold at most larger building centers. It includes (A) a new 200-amp panel; (B) a 200-amp bypass meter base (also called a socket); (C) individual circuit breakers (if your new panel is the same brand as your old ones you may be able to reuse the old breakers); (D) new, THW, THHW, THWN-2. RHW, RHW-2, XHHW (2/0 copper seen here); (E) 2" dia. rigid conduit; (F) weatherhead shroud for mast.

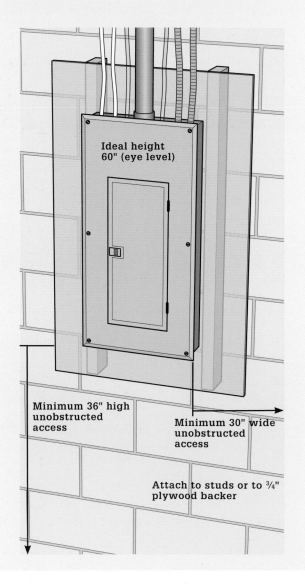

Ideal height 60" (eye level)

Minimum 36" high unobstructed access

Minimum 30" wide unobstructed access

Attach to studs or to ¾" plywood backer

Meter

Shutoff switch

A shutoff switch next to the electric meter is required if your main service panel is too far away from the point where the service cable enters your house. The maximum distance allowed varies widely, from as little as 3 ft. to more than 10 ft. Wiring the service cable through the shutoff has the effect of transforming your main service panel into a subpanel, which will impact how the neutral and ground wires are attached (see Subpanels, page 34).

How to Replace a Main Service Panel

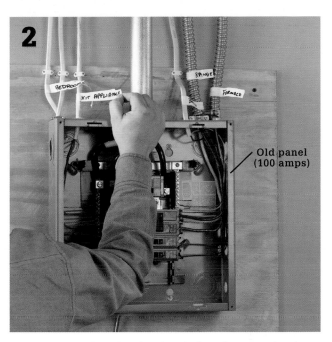

Shut off power to the house at the transformer. This must be done by a technician who is certified by your utility company. Also have the utility worker remove the old meter from the base. It is against the law for a homeowner to break the seal on the meter.

Label all incoming circuit wires before disconnecting them. Labels should be written clearly on tape that is attached to the cables outside of the existing service panel.

Disconnect incoming circuit wires from breakers, grounding bar, and neutral bus bar. Also disconnect cable clamps at the knockouts on the panel box. Retract all circuit wires from the service panel and coil up neatly, with the labels clearly visible.

Unscrew the lugs securing the service entry cables at the top of the panel. For 240-volt service, you will find two heavy-gauge SE cables, probably with black sheathing. Each cable carries 120 volts of electricity. A neutral service cable, usually of lighter gauge than the SE cables, will be attached to the neutral bus bar. This cable returns current to the source.

(continued)

5

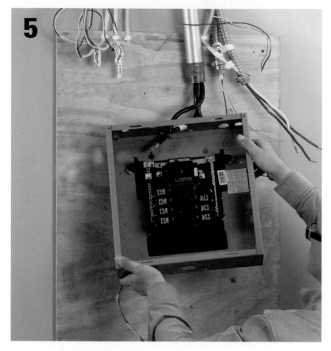

Remove the old service panel box. Boxes are rated for a range of power service; and if you are upgrading, the components in the old box will be undersized for the new service levels. The new box will have a greater number of circuit slots as well.

6

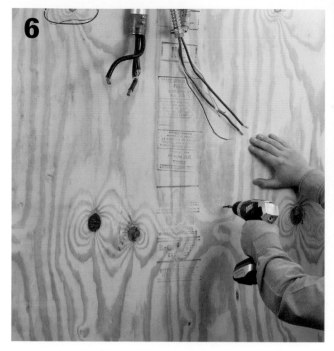

Replace the old panel backer board with a larger board in the installation area (see sidebar, page 40). A piece of ¾" plywood is typical. Make sure the board is well secured at wall framing members.

7

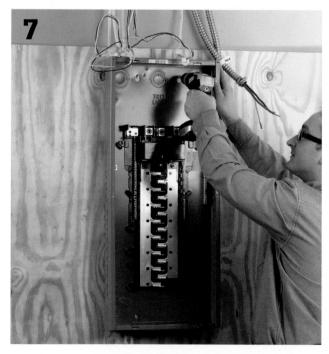

Attach the new service panel box to the backer board, making sure that at least two screws are driven through the backer and into wall studs. Drill clearance holes in the back of the box at stud locations if necessary. Use roundhead screws that do not have tapered shanks so the screwhead seats flat against the panel.

8

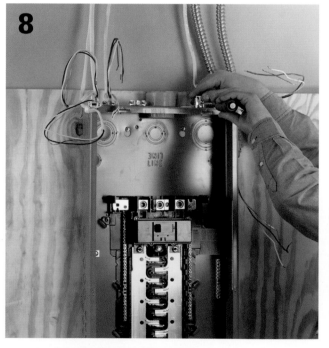

Attach properly sized cable clamps to the box at the knockout holes. Do not crowd multiple lines into a knockout hole, and plan carefully to avoid removing knockouts that you do not need to remove (if you do make a mistake, you can fill the knockout hole with a plug).

Splicing in the Box ▸

Some wiring codes allow you to make splices inside the service panel box if the circuit wire is too short. Use the correct wire cap and wind electrical tape over the conductors where they enter the cap. If your municipality does not allow splices in the panel box, you'll have to rectify a short cable by splicing it in a junction box before it reaches the panel, and then replacing the cable with a longer section for the end of the run. Make sure each circuit line has at least 12" of slack.

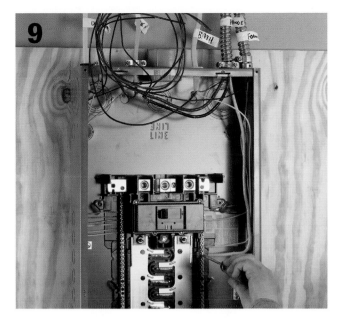

Attach the white neutral from each circuit cable to the neutral bus bar. Most panels have a preinstalled neutral bus bar, but in some cases you may need to purchase the bar separately and attach it to the panel back. The panel should also have a separate grounding bar that you may need to purchase separately. Attach the grounds as well. Do not attach more than one neutral wire to the same lug.

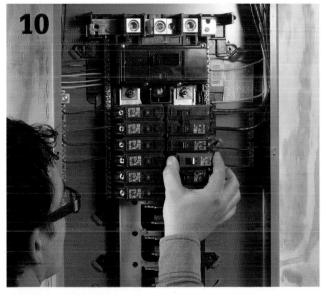

Attach the hot lead wire to the terminal on the circuit breaker and then snap the breaker into an empty slot. When loading slots, start at the top of the panel and work your way downward. It is important that you balance the circuits as you go to equalize the amperage. For example, do not install all the 15 amp circuits on one side and all the 20 amp circuits on the other. Also, if you have multiple larger-capacity circuits, such as a 50-amp dryer and a 50-amp range, do not install them on the same side of the panel in case they will be drawing electricity at the same time.

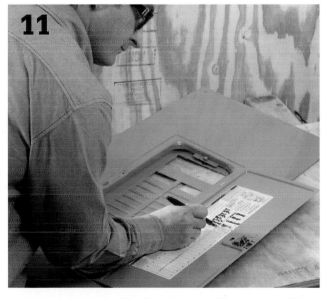

Create an accurate circuit index and affix it to the inside of the service panel door. List all loads that are on the circuit as well as the amperage. Once you have restored power to the new service panel (see step 18), test out each circuit to make sure you don't have any surprises. With the main breakers on, shut off all individual circuit breakers and then flip each one on by itself. Walk through your house and test every switch and receptacle to confirm the loads on that circuit.

(continued)

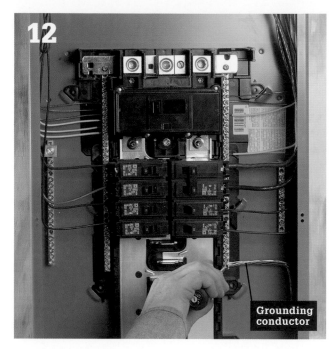

Install grounding conductors (see pages 46 to 51). Local codes are very specific about how the grounding needs to be accomplished. For example, some require multiple rods driven at least 6 ft. apart. Discuss your grounding requirements thoroughly with your inspector or an electrician before making your plan.

Grounding conductor

Replace the old meter base (have the utility company remove the meter when they shut off power to the house, step 1). Remove the old meter base, also called a socket, and install a new base that's rated for the amperage of your new power service. Here, a 200-amp bypass meter base is being installed.

Update the conduit that runs from your house to the bottom of the meter base. This should be 2" rigid conduit in good repair. Attach the conduit to the base and wall with the correct fittings. Rigid metal conduit is a good option, but Schedule 80 PVC is probably the best choice for housing the service entry cables.

Install new service entry wires. Each wire carries 120 volts of current from the meter to the service wire lugs at the top of your service panel. Code is very specific about how these connections are made. In most cases, you'll need to tighten the terminal nuts with a specific amount of torque that requires a torque wrench to measure. Also attach the sheathed neutral wire to the neutral/grounding lug.

16

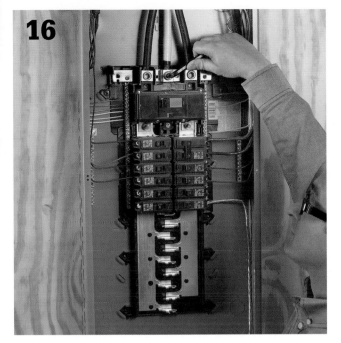

Attach the SE wires to the lugs connected to the main breakers at the top of your service entry panel. Do not remove too much insulation on the wires—leaving the wires exposed is a safety hazard. The neutral service entry wire is attached either directly to the neutral bus bar or to a metal bridge that is connected to the neutral bonding bus bar. Install the green grounding screw provided with the panel.

17

Install service entry wires from the meter to the weatherhead, where the connections to the power source are made. Only an agent for your public utility company may make the hookup at the weatherhead.

Tall Mast, Short Roof ▸

The service drop must occur at least 10 ft. above ground level, and as much as 14 ft. in some cases. Occasionally, this means that you must run the conduit for the service mast up through the eave of your roof and seal the roof penetration with a boot.

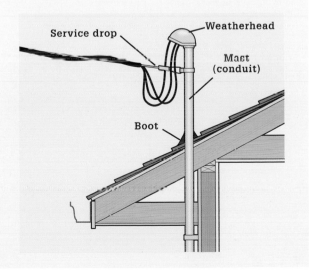

18

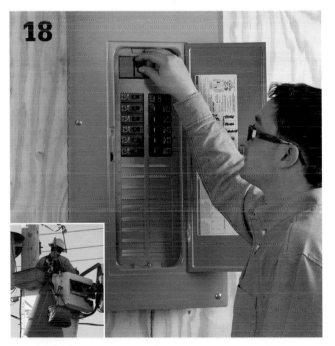

Have the panel and all connections inspected and approved by your local building department, and then contact the public utility company to make the connections at the power drop. Once the connections are made, turn the main breakers on and test all circuits.

Grounding & Bonding an Upgraded System

All home electrical supply systems must be bonded and grounded in accordance with code standards. This entails two tasks: the metal water and gas pipes must be connected electrically to create a contiguous wire path leading to a ground; and the main electrical panel must be grounded to a grounding rod or rods driven into the earth near the foundation of your house. Although the piping system often is bonded to the ground through your main electrical service panel, the panel grounding and the piping bonding are unrelated when it comes to function. The grounding wire that runs from your electrical panel to grounding rods in the earth is an important safeguard in your electrical system. The wires that bond and ground your metal piping are preventative, and they only become important in the relatively unlikely event that an electrical conductor contacts one of the bare pipes, energizing it. In that case, correct grounding of the piping system will ensure that the current does not remain or build up in the system, where it could electrocute anyone who touches a part of the system, such as a faucet handle. Bonding is done relatively efficiently at the water heater, as the gas piping and water piping generally there.

Tools & Materials ▸

Hammer	Cable staples
Slotted screwdriver	3 pipe ground clamps
Drill	Eye and ear protection
½" drill bit	Work gloves
Copperwire:	Grounding rods (8-ft.-
#4 stranded for	long copper-coated
100 amps and	steel)
above; #6 solid	5-lb. maul
for less than	Caulk
100 amps	

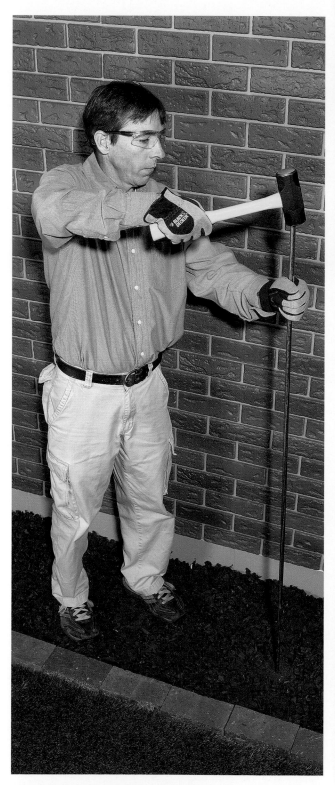

A pair of 8-ft.-long metal grounding rods are driven into the earth next to your house to provide a path to ground for your home wiring system.

How to Bond Metallic Piping

Determine the amperage rating of your electrical service by looking at your main breakers. The system amperage (usually 100 or 200 amps) determines the required gauge of the bonding wire you need. For service up to 125 amps use #8 copper strand wire. For more than 125 amps use #6 copper strand.

Run the grounding wire from a bonding point near your water heater (a convenient spot if you have a gas-fueled heater) to an exit point where the wire can be bonded to the grounding wire that leads to the exterior grounding rods. This is frequently done at the service panel. Run this wire as you would any other cable, leaving approximately 6 to 8 ft. of wire at the water heater. If you are running this wire through the ceiling joists, drill a ½" hole as close to the center as possible to not weaken the joist. Staple the wire every 4 ft. if running it parallel to the joists.

Install pipe ground clamps on each pipe (hot water supply, cold water supply, gas), roughly a foot above the water heater. Do not install clamps near a union or elbow because the tightening of the clamps could break or weaken soldered joints. Also make sure the pipes are free and clear of any paint, rust, or any other contaminant that may inhibit a good clean connection. Do not overtighten the clamps.

Route the ground wire through each clamp wire hole and then tighten the clamps onto the wire. Do not cut or splice the wire: The same wire should run through all clamps.

(continued)

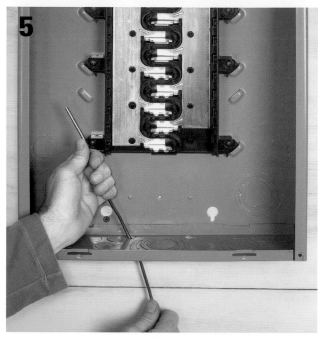

At the panel, turn off the main breaker. Open the cover by removing the screws and set the cover aside. Route the ground wire through a small ⅜" hole provided towards the rear of the panel on the top or bottom. You will generally have to knock the plug out of this hole by placing a screwdriver on it from the outside and tapping with a hammer. Make sure the ground wire will not come into contact with the copper bus bars in the middle of the panel or any of the load terminals on the breakers.

Locate an open hole on your ground and neutral bus and insert the ground wire. Newer service panels will have a separate neutral and grounding bus to conform to current codes in this case, connect to the grounding bus. These holes are large enough to accommodate up to a #4 awg wire, but it may be difficult at times. Secure the set screw at the lug. Replace the panel cover and turn the main breaker back on.

▌ Tips for Grounding the Panel

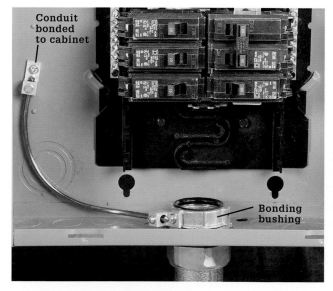

Neutral bus

Grounding bus

Conduit bonded to cabinet

Bonding bushing

The neutral and grounding wires should not be connected to the same bus in most subpanels. The grounding bus should be bonded to the subpanel cabinet. The neutral bus should not be bonded to the subpanel cabinet.

Metallic conduit must be physically and electrically connected to panel cabinets. A bonding bushing may be required in some cases, where all of a knockout is not removed.

Ground Rod Installation

The ground rod is an essential part of the grounding system. Its primary function is to create a path to ground for unrestricted electrical currents, such as lightning, line surges, and unintentional contact with high voltage lines. As a lot of homes are now being plumbed with nonmetallic pipes (which, unlike metallic pipes, cannot be used for equipment grounding), the need to properly install a grounding electrode system is more important than ever. In this day and age, only brand-new houses will have no grounding electrode system. However, it is not uncommon for electrodes to deteriorate in the ground and require replacement. Also, if you upgrade your electrical services you likely will need to upgrade your grounding wire and rods to meet code.

Note: Different municipalities have different requirements for grounding, so be sure to check with the AHJ *(Authority Having Jurisdiction)* first before attempting to do this yourself.

Call before you dig! Make sure the area where you will be installing the ground rods is free and clear from any underground utilities.

Exercise Your Breakers ▶

Your breakers (including the main) should be "exercised" once a year to ensure proper mechanical function. Simply turn them off and then back on. A convenient time to perform the exercise is at daylight savings time, when you'll need to reset all of your clocks anyway.

How to Install a Grounding Electrode System

Driving point

Striking face

Rim joist

Extended drill bit

First, determine what size ground rods you'll need: either ½" dia. by 8-ft. long for 100 amp service, or ⅝" dia. by 8-ft. long for services that exceed 100 amps. Grounding rods have a driving point on one end and a striking face on the other end. They are made of hardened, solid steel coated in copper for increased conductivity.

Drill a hole for the grounding conductor in the rim joist of your house, as close as practical to the main service panel. Drill all the way through to the outside of the house above the ground level at least 6" using an extended drill bit.

(continued)

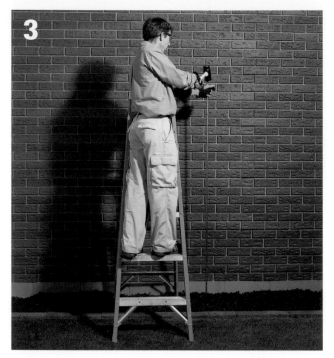

About a foot from the foundation of the house, pound one ground rod into the earth with a five-pound maul. If you encounter a rock or other obstruction, you can pound the ground rod at an angle as long as it does not exceed 45°. Drive until only 3" or 4" of the rod is above ground. Measure at least 6 ft. from the first ground rod and pound in another one.

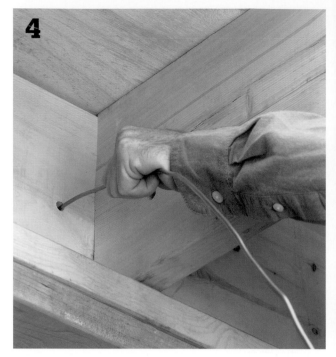

Run grounding conductor from the ground bus in your main service panel through the hole in the rim joist and to the exterior of the house, leaving enough wire to connect the two ground rods together. Make sure wire is sized correctly—see page 49.

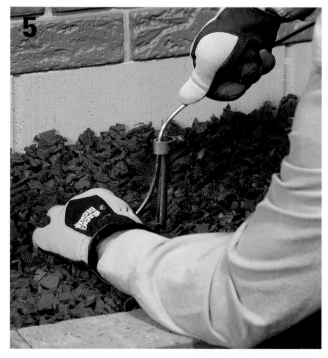

Using a brass connector commonly referred to as an acorn, connect the wire to the first ground rod, pulling the wire taut so no slack exists. Continue pulling the wire to reach the second grounding rod, creating a continuous connection.

Connect the second ground rod with another acorn to the uncut grounding wire previously pulled through the first acorn. Trim the excess wire.

7

8

Dig out a few inches around each rod to create clearance for the five-pound maul. Creating a shallow trench beneath the grounding wire between the rods is also a good idea. Drive each rod with the maul until the top of the rod is a few inches below grade.

Inject caulk into the hole in the rim joist on both the interior and exterior side.

Tips for Grounding

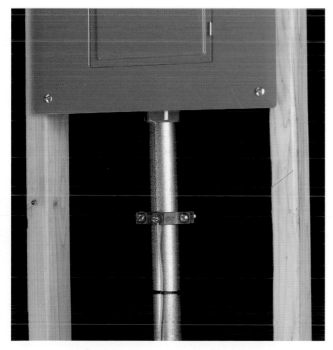

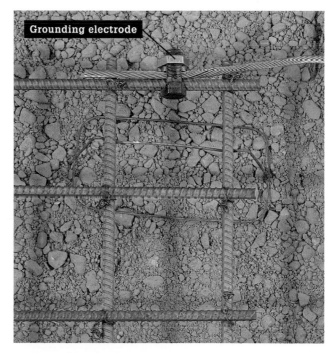

Grounding electrode

A listed metal strap may be used to ground indoor communication wires to bonded conduit such as telephone and cable TV.

A piece of reinforcing bar encased in a concrete footing is a common grounding electrode in new construction. Called a ufer, the electrode must be No. 4 or larger rebar and at least 20 ft. long. (Shown prior to pouring concrete.)

Adding Circuits

An electrical circuit is a continuous loop. Household circuits carry power from the main service panel, throughout the house, and back to the main service panel. Several switches, receptacles, light fixtures, or appliances may be connected to a single circuit.

Current enters a circuit loop on hot wires and returns along neutral wires. These wires are color coded for easy identification. Hot wires are black or red, and neutral wires are white or light gray. For safety, most circuits include a bare copper or green insulated grounding wire. The grounding wire conducts current in the event of a ground fault, and helps reduce the chance of severe electrical shock. The service panel also has a grounding wire connected to a metal water pipe and metal grounding rod buried underground.

If a circuit carries too much power, it can overload. A fuse or a circuit breaker protects each circuit in case of overloads.

Current returns to the service panel along a neutral circuit wire. Current then becomes part of a main circuit and leaves the house on a large neutral service wire that returns it to the utility pole transformer.

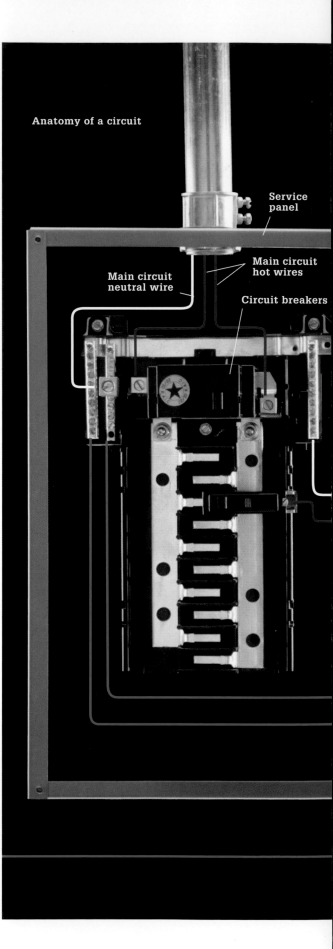

Anatomy of a circuit

Service panel

Main circuit hot wires

Main circuit neutral wire

Circuit breakers

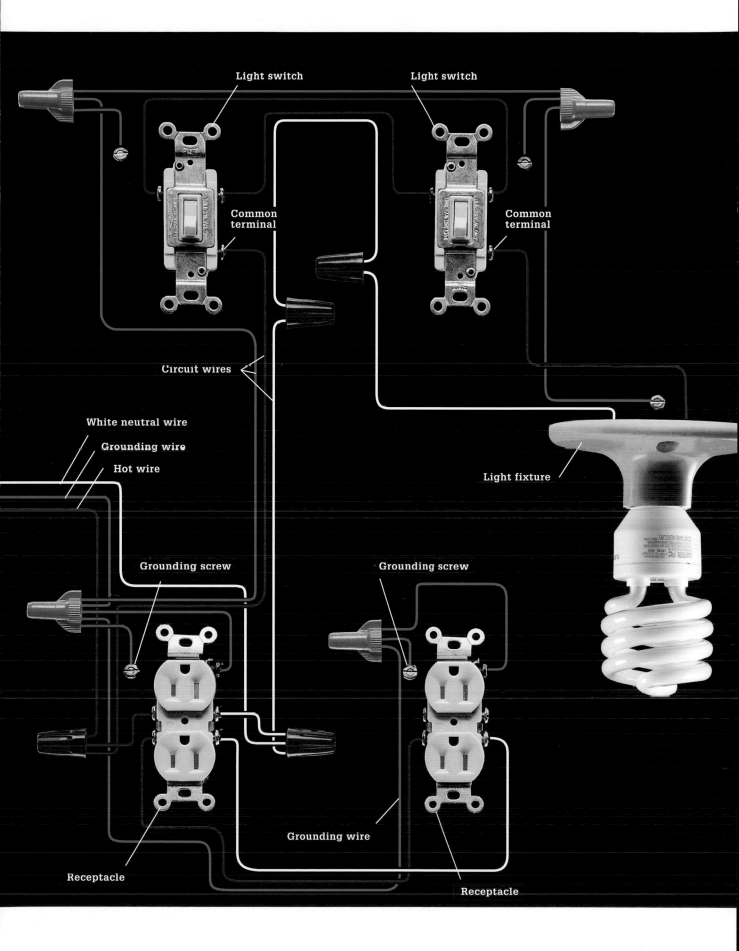

Light switch

Light switch

Common
terminal

Common
terminal

Circuit wires

White neutral wire

Grounding wire

Hot wire

Light fixture

Grounding screw

Grounding screw

Receptacle

Grounding wire

Receptacle

Wiring a Room Addition

The photo below shows the circuits you would likely want to install in a large room addition. This example shows the framing and wiring of an unfinished attic converted to an office or entertainment room with a bathroom. This room includes a subpanel and five new circuits plus telephone and cable-TV lines.

A wiring project of this sort is a potentially complicated undertaking that can be made simpler by breaking the project into convenient steps, and finishing one step before moving on to the next. Turn to pages 56 to 57 to see this project represented as a wiring diagram.

Individual Circuits

#1: Bathroom circuit. This 20-amp dedicated circuit supplies power to bathroom lights and fans, as well as receptacles that must be GFCI-protected at the box or at the receptacle. As with small appliance circuits in the kitchen, you may not tap into this circuit to feed any additional loads.

#2: Computer circuit. A 15-amp dedicated circuit with isolated ground is recommended, but an individual branch circuit is all that is required by most codes.

Circuit breaker subpanel receives power through a 10-gauge, three-wire feeder cable connected to a 30-amp,

14/2 cable

Vent fan

Vanity light fixture

GFCI rece

Circuit breaker subpanel

12/2 cable

12/2 cable

Time & light fixture swit

14/3 cable

Blower heater

10/3 cable

240-volt circuit breaker at the main circuit breaker panel. Larger room additions may require a 60-amp or a 100-amp feeder circuit breaker.

#3: Air-conditioner circuit. A 20-amp, 240-volt dedicated circuit. In cooler climates, or in a smaller room, you may need an air conditioner and circuit rated for only 120 volts.

#4: Basic lighting/receptacle circuit. This 15-amp, 120-volt circuit supplies power to most of the fixtures in the bedroom and study areas.

#5: Heater circuit. This 20-amp, 240-volt circuit supplies power to the bathroom blower-heater and to the baseboard heaters. Depending on the size of your room and the wattage rating of the baseboard heaters, you may need a 30-amp, 240-volt heating circuit.

Telephone outlet is wired with 22-gauge four-wire phone cable. If your home phone system has two or more separate lines, you may need to run a cable with eight wires, commonly called four-pair cable.

Cable television jack is wired with coaxial cable running from an existing television junction in the utility area.

14/3 cable

14/3 cable

Phone cable

Coaxial cable

These cables continue through the foreground wall to complete the circuits. This wall has been removed for clarity.

12/2 cable

14/2 cable

Diagram View

The diagram below shows the layout of the five circuits and the locations of their receptacles, switches, fixtures, and devices as shown in the photo on the previous pages. The circuits and receptacles are based on the needs of a 400-sq.-ft. space. An inspector will want to see a diagram like this one before issuing a permit. After you've received approval for your addition, the wiring diagram will serve as your guide as you complete your project.

■ **Circuit #1:** A 20-amp, 120-volt circuit serving the bathroom and closet area. Includes: 12/2 NM cable, double-gang box, timer switch, single-pole switch, 4 × 4″ box with single-gang adapter plate, two plastic light fixture boxes, vanity light fixture, closet light fixture, 15-amp single-pole circuit breaker.

■ **Circuit #2:** A 15-amp, 120-volt computer circuit. Includes: 14/2 NM cable, single-gang box, 15-amp receptacle, 15-amp single-pole circuit breaker.

■ **Circuit #3:** A 20-amp, 240-volt air-conditioner circuit. Includes: 12/2 NM cable; single-gang box;

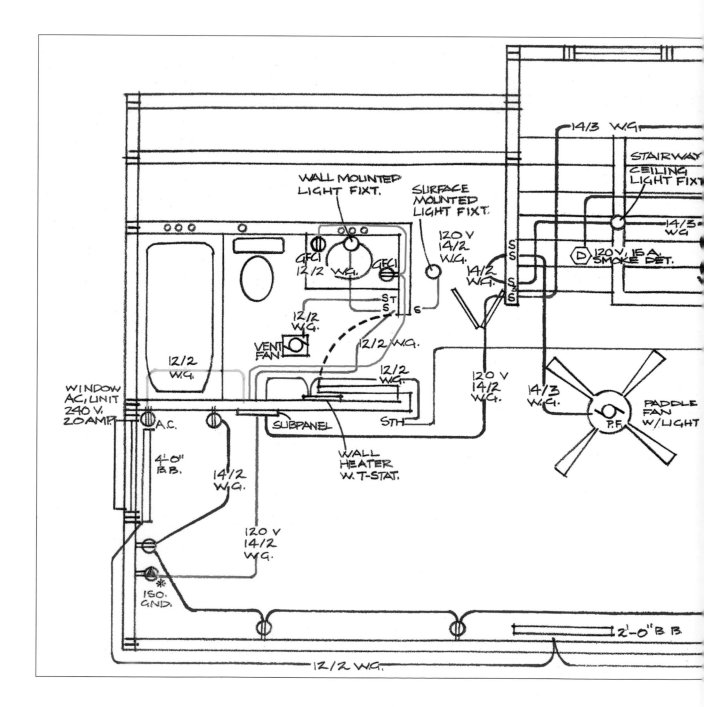

20-amp, 240-volt receptacle (singleplex style); 20-amp double-pole circuit.

Circuit #4: A 15-amp, 120-volt basic lighting/receptacle circuit serving most of the fixtures in the bedroom and study areas. Includes: 14/2 and 14/3 NM cable, two double-gang boxes, fan speed-control switch, dimmer switch, single-pole switch, two three-way switches, two plastic light fixture boxes, light fixture for stairway, smoke detector, metal light fixture box with brace bar, ceiling fan with light fixture, 10 single-gang boxes, 4" × 4" box with single-gang adapter plate, 10 duplex receptacles (15-amp), 15-amp single-pole circuit breaker.

Circuit #5: A 20-amp, 240-volt circuit that supplies power to three baseboard heaters controlled by a wall thermostat, and to a bathroom blower-heater controlled by a built-in thermostat. Includes: 12/2 NM cable, 750-watt blower heater, single-gang box, line-voltage thermostat, three baseboard heaters, 20-amp double-pole circuit breaker.

TV **Cable television jack:** Coaxial cable with F-connectors, signal splitter, cable television outlet with mounting brackets.

Circuit #6: A 20-amp, 120-volt, GFCI-protected bathroom receptacle circuit for the bathroom. Includes GFCI breaker, 12/2 NM cable, boxes and 20-amp receptacles.

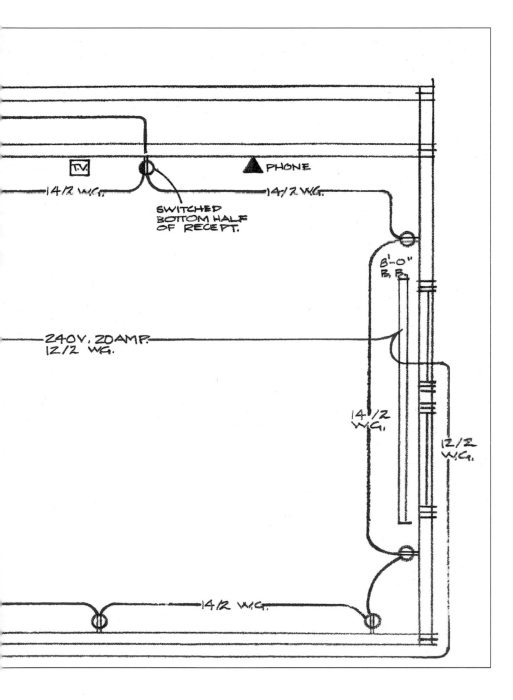

Circuit Map Details

Make the final connections for receptacles, switches, and fixtures only after the rough-in inspection is done, and all walls and ceilings are finished. The circuit maps are especially useful if your wiring configurations differ from those shown on the following pages. The last step is to hook up the new circuits at the breaker panel.

After all connections are done, your work is ready for the final inspection. If you have worked carefully, the final inspection will take only a few minutes. The inspector may open one or two electrical boxes to check wire connections, and will check the circuit breaker hookups to make sure they are correct.

Tools & Materials ▸

Combination tool
Screwdrivers
Needlenose pliers
Nut driver
Pigtail wires
Wire connectors
Green & black tape

CIRCUIT #1
A 15-amp, 120-volt circuit serving the bathroom & closet.

- Timer & single-pole switch
- Vent fan
- Two light fixtures
- GFCI receptacle
- Single-pole switch
- 15-amp single-pole circuit breaker

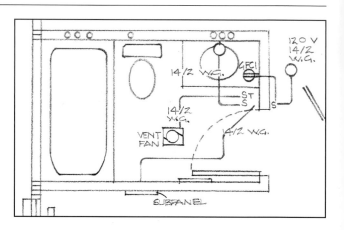

How to Connect the Timer & Single-pole Switch

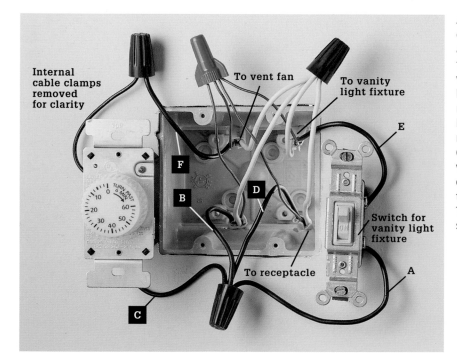

Attach a black pigtail wire (A) to one of the screw terminals on the switch. Use a wire connector to connect this pigtail to the black feed wire (B), to one of the black wire leads on the timer (C), and to the black wire carrying power to the bathroom receptacle (D). Connect the black wire leading to the vanity light fixture (E) to the remaining screw terminal on the switch. Connect the black wire running to the vent fan (F) to the remaining wire lead on the timer. Use wire connectors to join the white wires and the grounding wires. Tuck all wires into the box, then attach the switches, coverplate, and timer dial.

How to Connect a Vent Fan

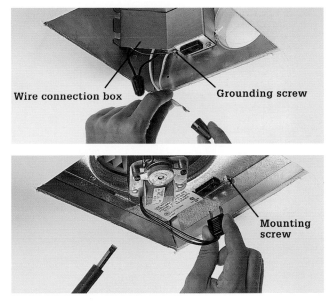

Wire connection box   Grounding screw

Mounting screw

In the wire connection box (top) connect black circuit wire to black wire lead on fan, using a wire connector. Connect white circuit wire to white wire lead. Connect grounding wire to the green grounding screw.

Insert the fan motor unit (bottom), and attach mounting screws. Connect the fan motor plug to the built-in receptacle on the wire connection box. Attach the fan grill to the frame, using the mounting clips included with the fan kit.

How to Connect Light Fixtures

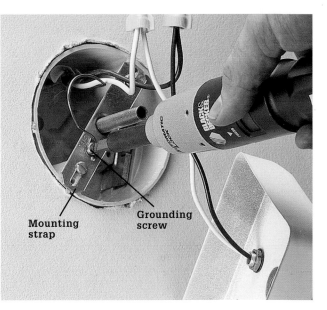

Mounting strap   Grounding screw

Attach a mounting strap with threaded nipple to the box, if required by the light fixture manufacturer. Connect the black circuit wire to the black wire lead on the light fixture, and connect the white circuit wire to the white wire lead. Connect the circuit grounding wire to the grounding screw on the mounting strap. Carefully tuck all wires into the electrical box, then position the fixture over the nipple, and attach it with the mounting nut.

How to Connect the Bathroom GFCI Receptacle

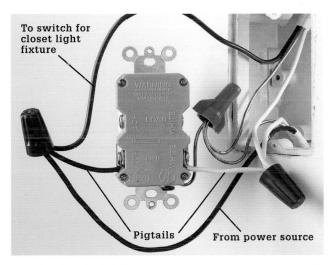

To switch for closet light fixture

Pigtails   From power source

Attach a black pigtail wire to brass screw terminal marked line. Join all black wires with a wire connector. Attach a white pigtail wire to the silver screw terminal marked line, then join all white wires with a wire connector. Attach a grounding pigtail to the green grounding screw, then join all grounding wires. Tuck all wires into the box, then attach the receptacle and the coverplate.

How to Connect the Single-pole Switch

Attach the black circuit wires to the brass screw terminals on the switch. Use wire connectors to join the white neutral wires together and the bare copper grounding wires together. Tuck all wires into the box, then attach the switch and the coverplate.

CIRCUIT #4
A 15-amp, 120-volt basic lighting/receptacle circuit serving the office and bedroom areas.

- Single-pole switch for split receptacle, three-way switch for stairway light fixture
- Speed-control and dimmer switches for ceiling fan
- Switched duplex receptacle
- 15-amp, 120-volt receptacles
- Ceiling fan with light fixture
- Smoke detector
- Stairway light fixture
- 15-amp single-pole circuit breaker

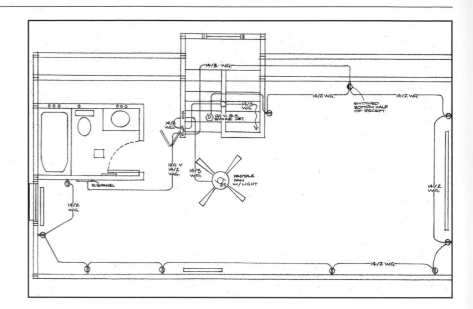

How to Connect Switches for Receptacle & Stairway Light

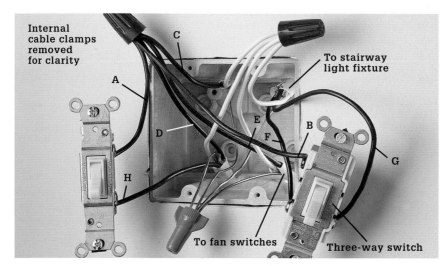

Attach a black pigtail wire (A) to one of the screws on the single-pole switch and another black pigtail (B) to common screw on three-way switch. Use a wire connector to connect pigtail wires to black feed wire (C), to black wire running to unswitched receptacles (D), and to the black wire running to fan switches (E). Connect remaining wires running to light fixture (F, G) to traveler screws on three-way switch. Connect red wire running to switched receptacle (H) to remaining screw on single-pole switch. Use wire connectors to join white wires and grounding wires. Tuck all wires into box, then attach switches and coverplate.

How to Connect the Ceiling Fan Switches

Connect the black feed wire (A) to one of the black wire leads on each switch, using a wire connector. Connect the red circuit wire (B) running to the fan light fixture to the remaining wire lead on the dimmer switch. Connect the black circuit wire (C) running to the fan motor to the remaining wire lead on the speed-control switch. Use wire connectors to join the white wires and the grounding wires. Tuck all wires into the box, then attach the switches, coverplate, and switch dials.

How to Connect a Switched Receptacle

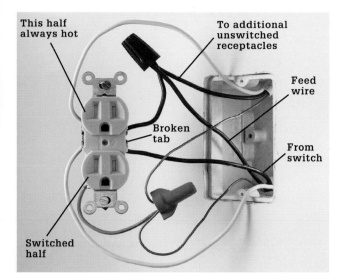

Break the connecting tab between the brass screw terminals on the receptacle, using needlenose pliers. Attach the red wire to the bottom brass screw. Connect a black pigtail wire to the other brass screw, then connect all black wires with a wire connector. Connect white wires to silver screws. Attach a grounding pigtail to the green grounding screw, then join all the grounding wires, using a wire connector. Tuck the wires into the box, then attach the receptacle and coverplate.

How to Connect Receptacles

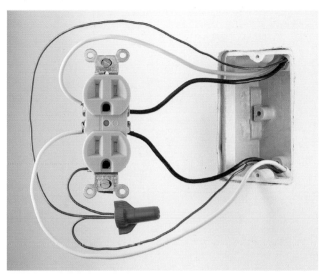

Connect the black circuit wires to the brass screw terminals on the receptacle, and the white wires to the silver terminals. Attach a grounding pigtail to the green grounding screw on the receptacle, then join all grounding wires with a wire connector. Tuck the wires into the box, then attach the receptacle and coverplate.

How to Connect a Ceiling Fan/Light Fixture

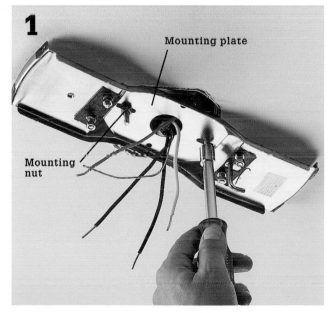

Place the ceiling fan mounting plate over the stove bolts extending through the electrical box. Pull the circuit wires through the hole in the center of the mounting plate. Attach the mounting nuts, and tighten them with a nut driver.

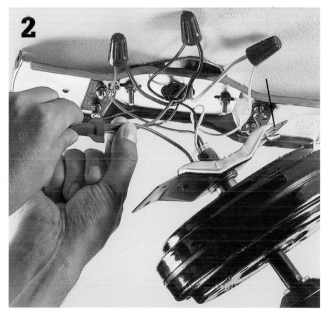

Hang fan motor from mounting hook. Connect black circuit wire to black wire lead from fan, using a wire connector. Connect red circuit wire from dimmer to blue wire lead from light fixture, white circuit wire to white lead, and grounding wires to green lead. Complete assembly of fan and light fixture, following manufacturer's directions.

■ CIRCUIT #5

A 20-amp, 240-volt circuit serving the bathroom blower-heater and three baseboard heaters controlled by a wall thermostat.

- 240-volt blower-heater
- 240-volt thermostat
- 240-volt baseboard heaters
- 20-amp double-pole circuit breaker (see pages 38 to 39 for instructions on hooking up the circuit at the circuit breaker panel)

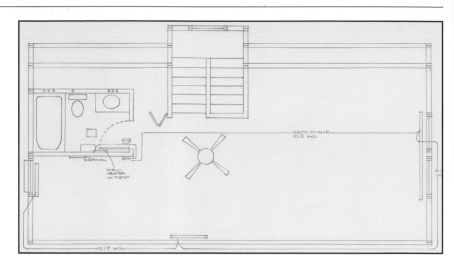

▌ How to Connect a 240-volt Blower-Heater

Motor unit
Motor plug
Wire connection box
Receptacle

Blower-heaters: In the heater's wire connection box, connect one of the wire leads to the white circuit wires, and the other wire lead to the black circuit wires, using same method as for baseboard heaters (page, opposite). Insert the motor unit, and attach the motor plug to the built-in receptacle. Attach the coverplate and thermostat knob. *Note: Some types of blower-heaters can be wired for either 120 volts or 240 volts. If you have this type, make sure the internal plug connections are configured for 240 volts.*

▌ How to Connect a 240-volt Thermostat

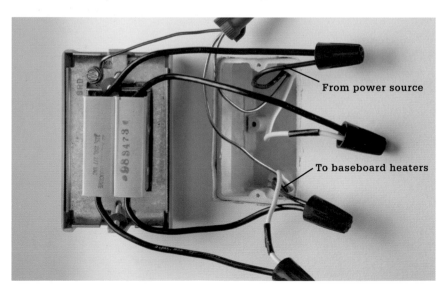

From power source
To baseboard heaters

Connect the red wire leads on the thermostat to the circuit wires entering the box from the power source, using wire connectors. Connect black wire leads to circuit wires leading to the baseboard heaters. Tag the white wires with black tape to indicate they are hot. Attach a grounding pigtail to the grounding screw on the thermostat, then connect all grounding wires. Tuck the wires into the box, then attach the thermostat and coverplate. Follow manufacturer's directions: the color coding for thermostats may vary.

How to Connect 240-volt Baseboard Heaters

1

At the cable location, cut a small hole in the wallboard, 3" to 4" above the floor, using a wallboard saw. Pull the cables through the hole, using a piece of stiff wire with a hook on the end. Middle-of-run heaters will have 2 cables, while end-of-run heaters have only 1 cable.

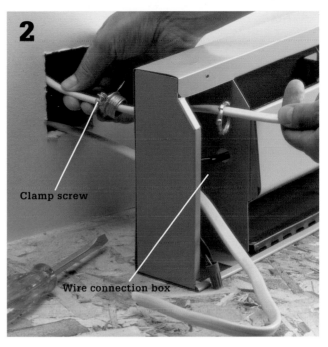

2

Clamp screw

Wire connection box

Remove the cover on the wire connection box. Open a knockout for each cable that will enter the box, then feed the cables through the cable clamps and into the wire connection box. Attach the clamps to the wire connection box and tighten the clamp screws until the cables are gripped firmly.

3

Anchor heater against wall, about 1" off floor, by driving flat-head screws through back of housing and into studs. Strip away cable sheathing so at least ¼" of sheathing extends into the heater. Strip ¾" of insulation from each wire, using a combination tool.

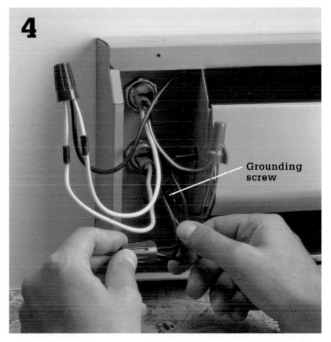

4

Grounding screw

Use wire connectors to connect the white circuit wires to one of the wire leads on the heater. Tag white wires with black tape to indicate they are hot. Connect the black circuit wires to the other wire lead. Connect a grounding pigtail to the green grounding screw in the box, then join all grounding wires with a wire connector. Reattach cover.

Wiring a Kitchen

14/2 cable

14/2 cable

12/3 cable

12/2 cable

6/3 cable

14/3 cable

14/2 cable

14/2 cable

12/3 cable

12/3 cable

14/2 cable

The photo at left shows the circuits you would probably want to install in a total kitchen remodel. Kitchens require a wide range of electrical services, from simple 15-amp lighting circuits to 120/240, 50-amp appliance circuits. This kitchen example has seven circuits, including separate dedicated circuits for a dishwasher and food disposer. Some codes allow the disposer and dishwasher to share a single circuit.

All rough carpentry and plumbing should be in place before beginning any electrical work. As always, divide a project of this scale into manageable steps, and finish one step before moving on. Turn to pages 66 to 67 to see this project represented as a wiring diagram.

Individual Circuits

■ **#1 & #2: Small-appliance circuits.** Two 20-amp, 120-volt circuits supply power to countertop and eating areas for small appliances. All general-use receptacles must be on these circuits. One 12/3 cable fed by a 20-amp double-pole breaker wires both circuits. These circuits share one electrical box with the disposer circuit (#5), and another with the basic lighting circuit (#7). Other circuits may also service the area, as with a dedicated refrigerator circuit.

■ **#3: Range circuit.** A 40- or 50-amp, 120/240-volt dedicated circuit supplies power to the range/ oven appliance. It is wired with 6/3 copper cable.

■ **#4: Microwave circuit.** It is wired with 12/2 cable. Microwaves that use less than 300 watts can be installed on a 15-amp circuit or plugged into the small-appliance circuits.

■ **#5: Food disposer/dishwasher circuit.** A dedicated 15-amp, 120-volt circuit supplies power to the disposer. It is wired with 14/2 cable. Some local codes may allow disposer to be on the same circuit as the dishwasher if it is a 20-amp circuit.

■ **#6: Basic lighting circuit.** A 15-amp, 120-volt circuit powers the ceiling fixture, recessed fixtures, and undercabinet task lights. 14/2 and 14/3 cables connect the fixtures and switches in the circuit. Each task light has a self-contained switch.

Diagram View

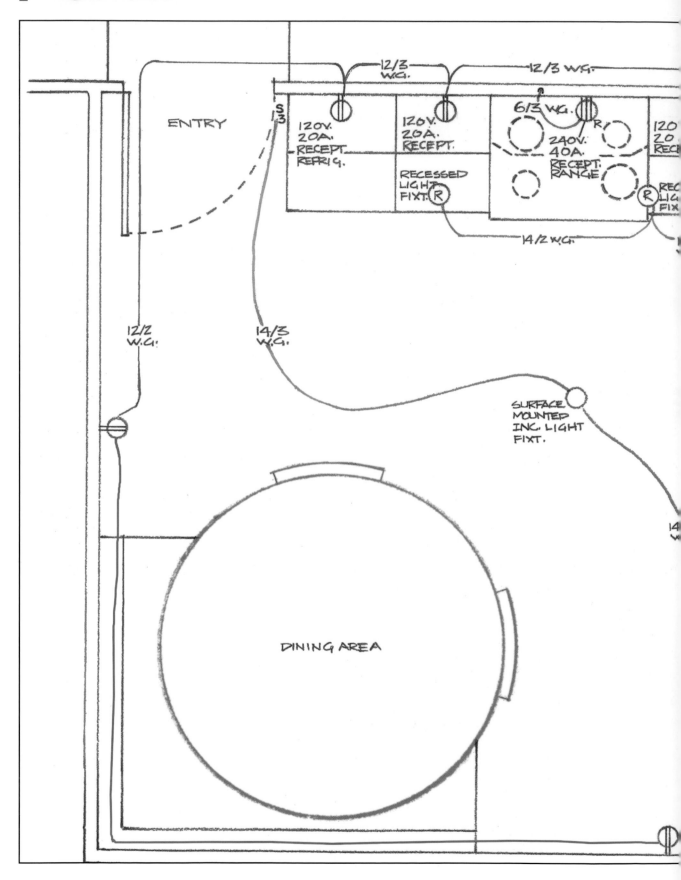

ENTRY

S
3

12/3 WG.

12/3 WG.

120V. 20A. RECEPT. REFRIG.

120V. 20A. RECEPT.

RECESSED LIGHT FIXT. R

6/3 WG.

R

240V. 40A. RECEPT. RANGE

120 20 REC

R REC LIG FIX

14/2 WG.

12/2 W.G.

14/3 W.G.

SURFACE MOUNTED INC. LIGHT FIXT.

14

DINING AREA

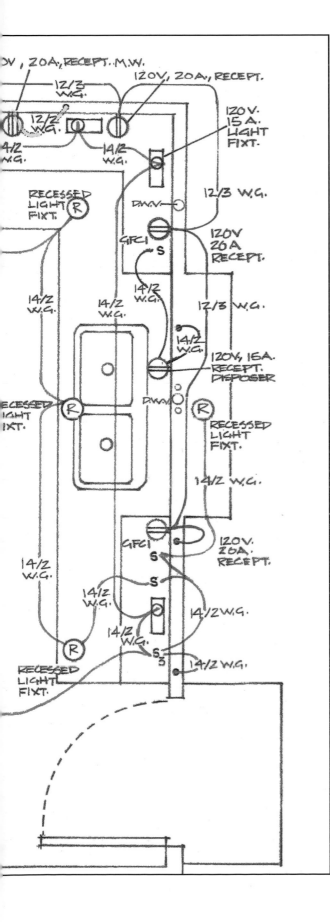

The diagram at left shows the layout of the seven circuits and the locations of their receptacles, switches, fixtures, and devices as shown in the photo on the previous pages. The circuits and receptacles are based on the needs of a 175-sq.-ft. space kitchen. An inspector will want to see a diagram like this one before issuing a permit. After you've received approval for your addition, the wiring diagram will serve as your guide as you complete your project.

■ **Circuits #1 & #2:** Two 20-amp, 120-volt small-appliance circuits wired with one cable. All general-use receptacles must be on these circuits, and they must be GFCI units. Includes: two GFCI receptacles rated for 20 amps, five electrical boxes that are 4 × 4", and 12/3 cable.

■ **Circuit #3:** A 50-amp, 120/240-volt dedicated circuit for the range. Includes: a 4 × 4" box; a 120/240-volt, 50-amp range receptacle; and 6/3 NM copper cable.

■ **Circuit #4:** A 20-amp, 120-volt dedicated circuit for the microwave. Includes: a 20-amp duplex receptacle, a single-gang box, and 12/2 NM cable.

■ **Circuit #5:** A 15-amp, 120-volt dedicated circuit for the food disposer. Includes: a 15-amp duplex receptacle, a single-pole switch (installed in a double-gang box with a GFCI receptacle from the small-appliance circuits), one single-gang box, and 14/2 cable.

■ **Circuit #6:** A 15-amp, 120-volt basic lighting circuit serving all of the lighting needs in the kitchen. Includes: two single-pole switches, two three-way switches, single-gang box, 4 × 4" box, triple-gang box (shared with one of the GFCI receptacles from the small-appliance circuits), plastic light fixture box with brace, ceiling light fixture, four fluorescent undercabinet light fixtures, six recessed light fixtures, 14/2 and 14/3 cables.

Making Connections

Make the final connections for switches, receptacles, and fixtures after the rough-in inspection. First make final connections on recessed fixtures (it is easier to do this before wallboard is installed). Then finish the work on walls and ceiling, install the cabinets, and make the rest of the final connections. Use the photos on the following pages and the circuit maps as a guide for making the final connections. The last step is to connect the circuits at the breaker panel. After all connections are made, your work is ready for the final inspection.

Tools & Materials ▸

Pigtail wires
Wire connectors

Black electrical tape

◼ CIRCUITS #1 & #2
Two 20-amp, 120-volt small-appliance circuits.

- 2 GFCI receptacles
- 20-amp double-pole circuit breaker

Note: *In this project, two of the GFCI receptacles are installed in boxes that also contain switches from other circuits (page opposite).*

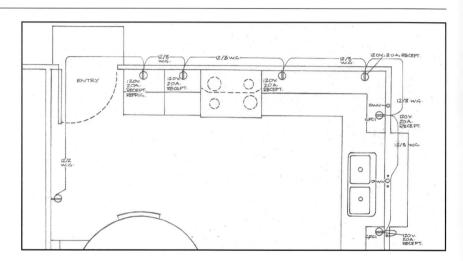

◼ How to Connect Small-appliance Receptacles (two alternating 20-amp circuits in one 12/3 cable)

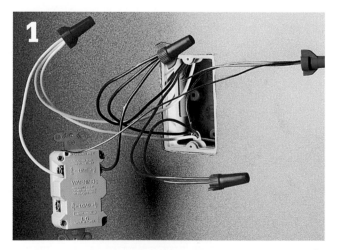

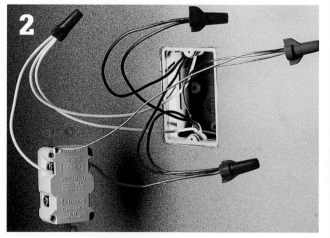

At alternate receptacles in the cable run (first, third, etc.), attach a black pigtail to a brass screw terminal marked line on the receptacle and to black wire from both cables. Connect a white pigtail to a silver screw (line) and to both white wires. Connect a grounding pigtail to the grounding screw and to both grounding wires. Connect both red wires together. Tuck wires into box, then attach the receptacle and coverplate.

At remaining receptacles in the run, attach a red pigtail to a brass screw terminal (line) and to red wires from the cables. Attach a white pigtail to a silver screw terminal (line) and to both white wires. Connect a grounding pigtail to the grounding screw and to both grounding wires. Connect both black wires together. Tuck wires into box, attach receptacle and coverplate.

How to Install a GFCI & a Disposer Switch

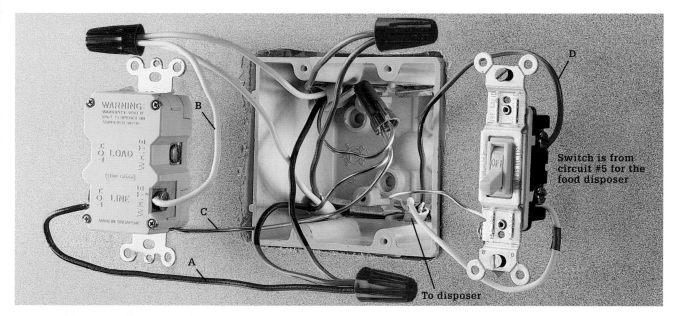

Connect black pigtail (A) to GFCI brass terminal marked line, and to black wires from three-wire cables. Attach white pigtail (B) to silver terminal marked line, and to white wires from three-wire cables. Attach grounding pigtail (C) to GFCI grounding screw and to grounding wires from three-wire cables. Connect both red wires together. Connect black wire from two-wire cable (D) to one switch terminal. Attach white wire to other terminal, and tag it black indicating it is hot. Attach grounding wire to switch grounding screw. Tuck wires into box; attach switch, receptacle, and coverplate.

How to Install a GFCI & Two Switches for Recessed Lights

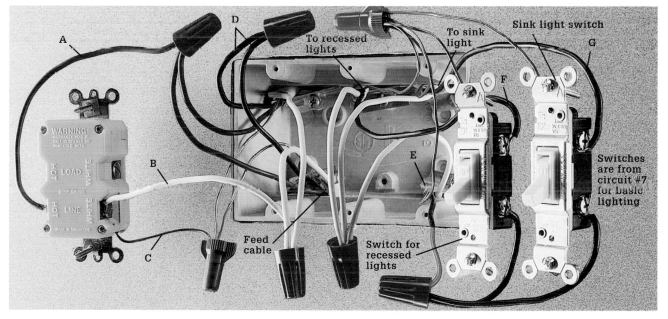

Connect red pigtail (A) to GFCI brass terminal labeled line, and to red wires from three-wire cables. Connect white pigtail (B) to silver line terminal and to white wires from three-wire cables. Attach grounding pigtail (C) to grounding screw and to grounding wires from three-wire cables. Connect black wires from three-wire cables (D) together. Attach a black pigtail to one screw on each switch and to black wire from two-wire feed cable (E). Connect black wire (F) from the two-wire cable leading to recessed lights to remaining screw on the switch for the recessed lights. Connect black wire (G) from two-wire cable leading to sink light to remaining screw on sink light switch. Connect white wires from all two-wire cables together. Connect pigtails to switch grounding screws and to all grounding wires from two-wire cables. Tuck wires into box; attach switches, receptacle, and coverplate.

CIRCUIT #3
A 50-amp, 120/240-volt circuit serving the range.

- 50-amp receptacle for range
- 50-amp double-pole circuit breaker

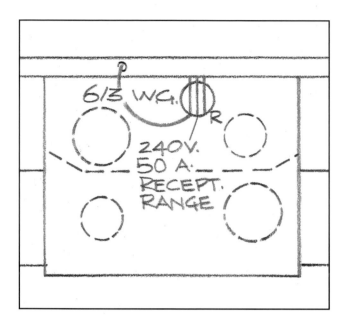

How to Install 120/240 Range Receptacle

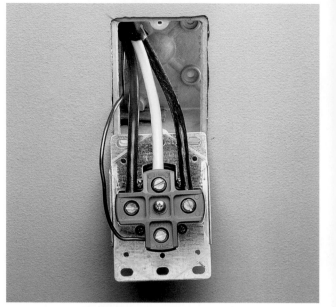

Attach the white wire to the neutral terminal and the black and red wires to the remaining terminals. Attach the bare copper grounding wire to the grounding screw on the receptacle. Attach receptacle and coverplate.

CIRCUIT #4
A 20-amp, 120-volt circuit for the microwave.

- 20-amp duplex receptacle
- 20-amp single-pole circuit breaker

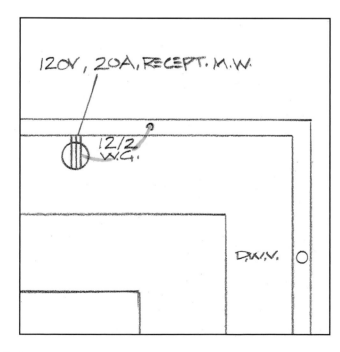

How to Connect Microwave

Connect black wire from the cable to a brass screw terminal on the receptacle. Attach the white wire to a silver screw terminal and the grounding wire to the receptacle's grounding screw. Tuck wires into box, then attach the receptacle and the coverplate.

A 15-amp, 120-volt circuit for the food disposer.

- 15-amp duplex receptacle
- Single-pole switch
- 15-amp single-pole circuit breaker

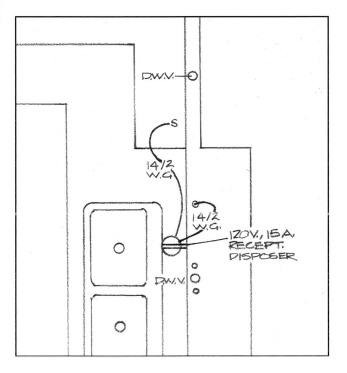

How to Connect Disposer Receptacle

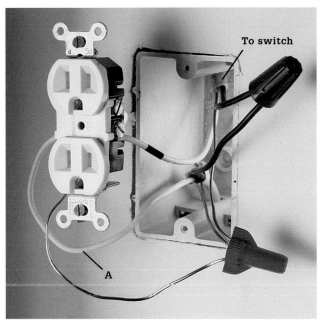

Connect black wires together. Connect white wire from feed cable (A) to silver screw on receptacle. Connect white wire from cable going to the switch to a brass screw terminal on the receptacle, and tag the wire with black indicating it is hot. Attach a grounding pigtail to grounding screw and to both cable grounding wires. Tuck wires into box, then attach receptacle and coverplate.

Circuit #5 Option:

A 20-amp, 120-volt circuit for disposer and dishwasher.

- 20-amp duplex receptacles
- 20-amp single-pole circuit breaker

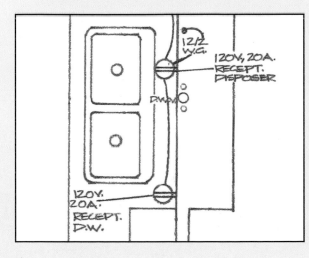

Connect the black wire to a brass screw terminal. Attach the white wire to a silver screw terminal. Connect the grounding wire to the grounding screw. Tuck wires into box, then attach receptacle and coverplate.
Note: Appliances with high amperage ratings may not be suitable for this configuration. Check with your local electrical inspector.

A 15-amp basic lighting circuit serving the kitchen.

- 2 three-way switches with grounding screws
- 2 single-pole switches with grounding screws
- Ceiling light fixture
- 6 recessed light fixtures
- 4 fluorescent under-cabinet fixtures
- 15-amp single-pole circuit breaker

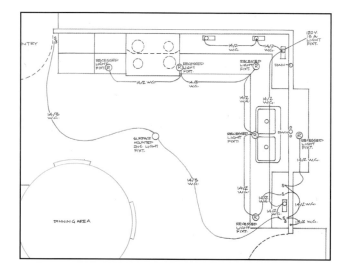

How to Connect First Three-way Switch

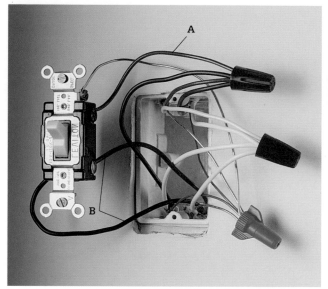

Connect a black pigtail to the common screw on the switch (A) and to the black wires from the two-wire cable. Connect black and red wires from the three-wire cable to traveler terminals (B) on the switch. Connect white wires from all cables entering box together. Attach a grounding pigtail to switch grounding screw and to all grounding wires in box. Tuck wires into box, then attach switch and coverplate.

How to Connect Surface-mounted Ceiling Fixture

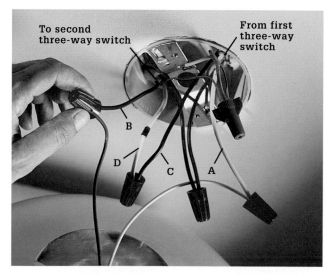

Connect white fixture lead to white wire (A) from first three-way switch. Connect black fixture lead to black wire (B) from second three-way switch. Connect black wire (C) from first switch to white wire (D) from second switch, and tag this white wire with black. Connect red wires from both switches together. Connect all grounding wires together. Mount fixture following manufacturer's instructions.

How to Connect Second Three-way Switch

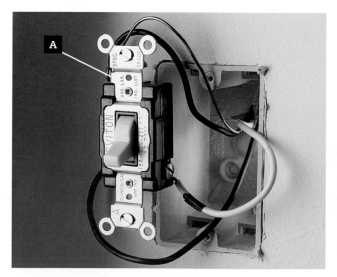

Connect black wire from the cable to the common screw terminal (A). Connect red wire to one traveler screw terminal. Attach the white wire to the other traveler screw terminal and tag it with black indicating it is hot. Attach the grounding wire to the grounding screw on the switch. Tuck wires in box, then attach switch and coverplate.

Installing Undercabinet Lights ▸

1

Drill ⅝" holes through wall and cabinet at locations that line up with knockouts on the fixture, and retrieve cable ends.

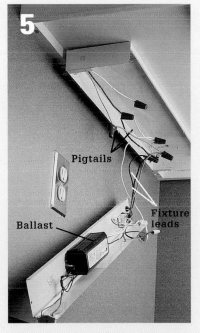

2

Remove access cover on fixture. Open one knockout for each cable that enters fixture box, and install cable clamps.

3

Strip 8" of sheathing from each cable end. Insert each end through a cable clamp, leaving ¼" of sheathing in fixture box.

4

Pigtails

Screw fixture box to cabinet. Attach black, white, and green pigtails of THHN/THWN wire to wires from one cable entering box. Pigtails must be long enough to reach the cable at other end of box.

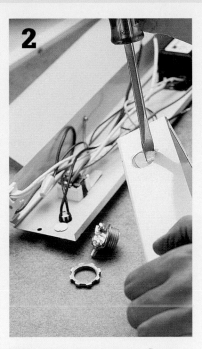

5

Pigtails

Ballast

Fixture leads

Connect black pigtail and circuit wire to black lead from fixture. Connect white pigtail and circuit wire to white lead from fixture. Attach green pigtail and copper circuit wire to green grounding wire attached to the fixture box.

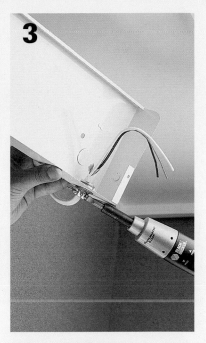

6

Tuck wires into box, and route THHN/THWN pigtails along one side of the ballast. Replace access cover and fixture lens.

Installing a Solar Light Circuit

A self-contained electrical circuit with dedicated loads, usually 12-volt light fixtures, is one of the most useful solar amenities you can install. A standalone system is not tied into your power grid, which greatly reduces the danger of installing the components yourself. Plus, the fact that your light fixtures are independent of the main power source means that even during a power outage you will have functioning emergency and security lights.

Installing a single solar-powered circuit is relatively simple, but don't take the dangers for granted. Your work will require permits and inspections in most jurisdictions, and you can't expect to pass if the work is not done to the exact specifications required.

Solar panels that convert the sun's energy into electricity are called photovoltaic (PV) panels,

and they produce direct current (DC) power. PV solar panel systems can be small and designed to accomplish a specific task, or they can be large enough to provide power or supplementary power to an entire house. Before you make the leap into a large system, it's a good idea to familiarize yourself with the mechanics of solar power. The small system demonstrated in this project is relatively simple and is a great first step into the world of solar. The fact that the collector, battery, and lights are a standalone system makes this a very easy project to accomplish. By contrast, installing panels that provide direct supplementary power through your main electrical service panel is a difficult wiring job that should be done by professional electricians only.

This 60-watt solar panel is mounted on a garage roof and powers a self-contained home security lighting system. Not only does this save energy costs, it keeps the security lights working even during power outages.

Schematic Diagram for an Off-the-Grid Solar Lighting System

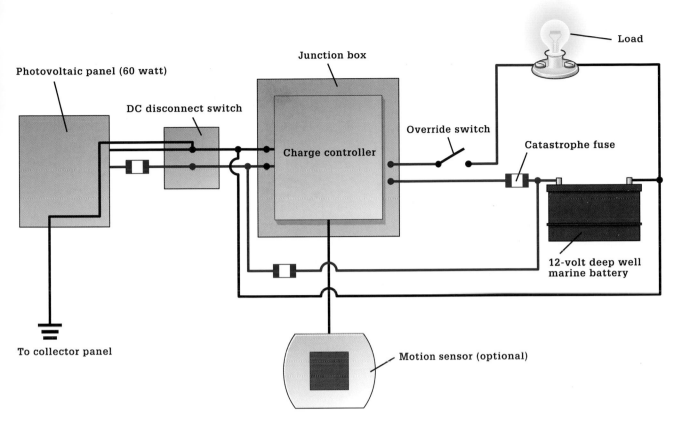

Photovoltaic panel (60 watt)

DC disconnect switch

Junction box

Charge controller

Override switch

Catastrophe fuse

Load

12-volt deep well marine battery

To collector panel

Motion sensor (optional)

Tools & Materials ▸

Tape measure
Drill/driver with bits
Caulk gun
Crimping tool
Wiring tools
Metal-cutting saw
Photovoltaic panel
  (50 to 80 watts)
Charge controller
Catastrophe fuse
Battery sized for
  3 day autonomy
Battery case
Battery cables
12 volt LED lights
  including motion-
  sensor light
Additional 12-volt light
  fixtures as desired

20 ft. Unistrut 1⅞"
  thick U-channel (See
  Resources, page 125)
(4) 45° Unistrut
  connectors
(2) 90° Unistrut
  angle brackets
(4) Unistrut hold
  down clamps
(12) ⅜" spring nuts
(12) ⅜"-dia. × 1"-long
  hex-head bolts
  with washers
DC-rated disconnect
  or double throw
  snap switch
6" length of ½"-dia.
  liquid-tight flexible
  metallic conduit

(2) ½" liquid
  tight connectors
(2) Lay-in
  grounding lugs
(2) Insulated terminal
  bars to accept one
  2-gauge wire and
  4 12-gauge wires
(2) Cord cap
  connectors for
  ½"-dia. cable
½" ground rod
  and clamp
Copper wire
  (6, 12-gauge)
Green ground screws
½" Flexible metallic
  conduit or
  Greenfield

½" Greenfield
  connectors
(4) ¹¹⁄₁₆" junction boxes
  with covers
(4) square boxes
  with covers
PVC 6 × 6" junction
  box with cover
14/2 UF wire
¼ × 20 nuts and bolts
  with lock washers
Roof flashing boot
Roof cement
Silicon caulk
Eye protection

Mounting PV Panels

The mounting stand for the PV panel is constructed from metal U-channel (a product called Unistrut is seen here. See Resources page 125) and pre-bent fasteners. Position the solar panel where it will receive the greatest amount of sunlight for the longest period of time each day—typically the south-facing side of a roof or wall. For a circuit with a battery reserve that powers two to four 12-volt lights, a collection panel rated between 40 and 80 watts of output should suffice. These panels can range from $200 to $600 in price, depending on the output and the overall quality.

The stand components are held together with bolts and spring-loaded fasteners. The 45° and 90° connectors are manufactured specifically for use with this Unistrut system.

Connections for the feed wires that carry current from the collector are made inside an electrical box mounted on the back of the collector panel.

An EPDM rubber boot seals off the opening where the PVC conduit carrying the feed wires penetrates the roof.

How to Wire a DC Lighting Circuit

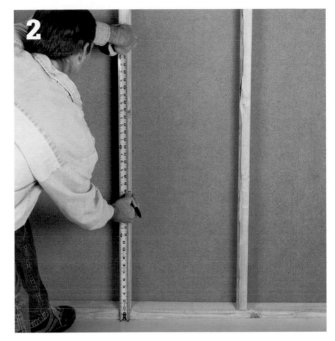

Mount a junction box inside the building where the conduit and wiring enter from the power source. Secure the box to the conduit with appropriate connectors. Run two #14 awg wires through the conduit and connect them to the positive and negative terminals on the panel.

Plan the system layout. Determine the placement of the battery and then decide where you will position the charge controller and DC disconnect. The battery should be placed at least 18" off the floor, in a well ventilated area where it won't be agitated by everyday activity. Mark locations directly on the wall.

Attach a junction box for enclosing the DC disconnect, which is a heavy-duty switch, to a wall stud near the battery and charge controller location. Use a metal single-gang box with mounting flanges.

Run flexible metal conduit from the entry point at the power source to the junction box for the DC disconnect box. Use hangers rated for flexible conduit.

(continued)

Attach a double gang metal junction box to the building's frame beneath the DC disconnect box to enclose the charge controller. Connect the boxes with a suitable conduit fitting or with flexible conduit.

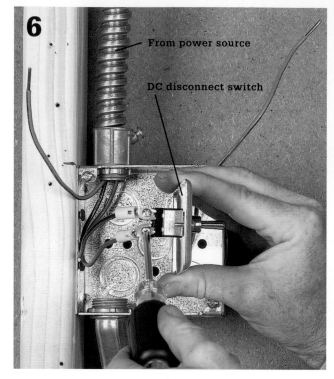

From power source

DC disconnect switch

Attach the DC disconnect switch to the wire leads from the power source.

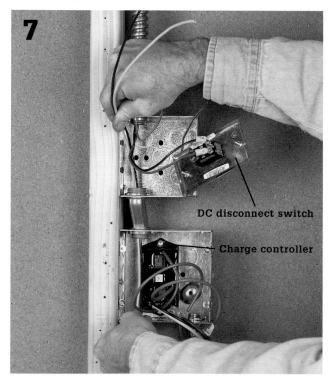

DC disconnect switch

Charge controller

Install the charge controller inside the box.

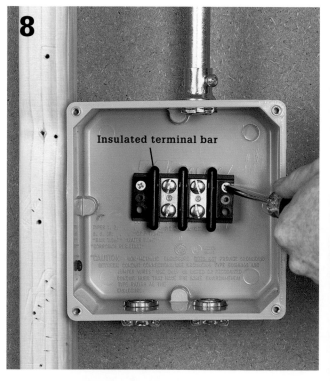

Insulated terminal bar

Mount a PVC junction box for the battery controller about 2 ft. above the battery location and install an insulated terminal bar within the box.

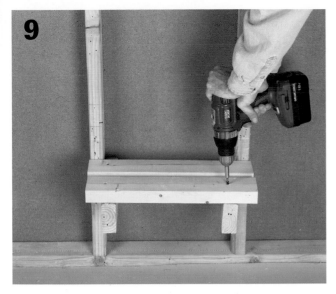

Build a support shelf for the battery. The shelf should be at least 12" to 18" above ground. Set the battery on the shelf in a sturdy plastic case.

Set up grounding protection. Pound an 8-ft. long, ½"-dia. ground rod into the ground outside the building, about 1 ft. from the wall on the opposite side of the charge controller. Leave about 2" of the rod sticking out of the ground. Attach a ground rod clamp to the top of the rod. Drill a 5/16" hole through the wall (underneath a shake or siding piece) and run the #6-gauge THWN wire to the ground rod. This ground will facilitate lightning protection. See pages 46 to 51 for more information on grounding the system.

Wire the DC disconnect. Attach the two #14-gauge wires to the two terminals labeled "line" on the top of the DC disconnect switch.

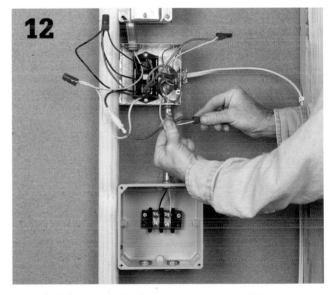

Wire the charge controller. Route two more #14-gauge wires from the bottom of the DC disconnect terminals into the 4 × 11/16 junction box and connect to the "Solar Panel In" terminals on the charge controller. The black wire should connect to the negative terminal in the PVC box and the red to the positive lead on the charge controller. Finish wiring of the charge controller according to the line diagram provided with the type of controller purchased. Generally the load wires connect to the orange lead and the red wire gets tied to the battery through a fuse.

(continued)

Option: Attach a motion sensor. Some charge controllers come equipped with a motion sensor to maximize the efficiency of your lighting system—these are especially effective when used with security lighting. The motion sensor is typically mounted to a bell box outside and wired directly to the charge controller with an 18-gauge × 3-conductor insulated cable. A system like this can support up to three motion sensors. Follow the manufacturer's directions for installing and wiring the motion sensor.

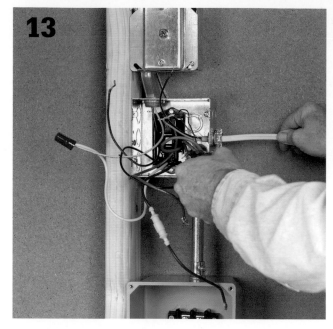

13

Run wiring to the loads (exterior DC lighting fixtures in this case) from the charge controller. DC light fixtures (12-volt) with LED bulbs can be purchased at marine and RV stores if you can't find them in your home center or electrical supply store.

14

Install the battery. Here, a deep-cell 12-volt marine battery is used. First, cut and strip each of the two battery cables at one end and install into the battery control junction box through cord cap connectors. Terminate these wires on two separate, firmly mounted insulated terminal blocks.

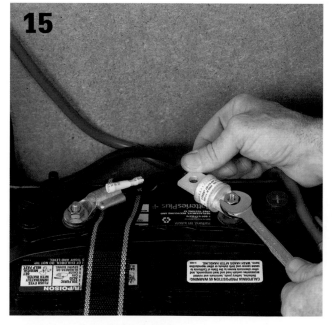

15

Install the catastrophe fuse onto the positive terminal using nuts and bolts provided with the battery cables. Connect the battery cables to the battery while paying close attention to the polarity (red to positive and black to negative). Make sure all connections have been made and double check.

16

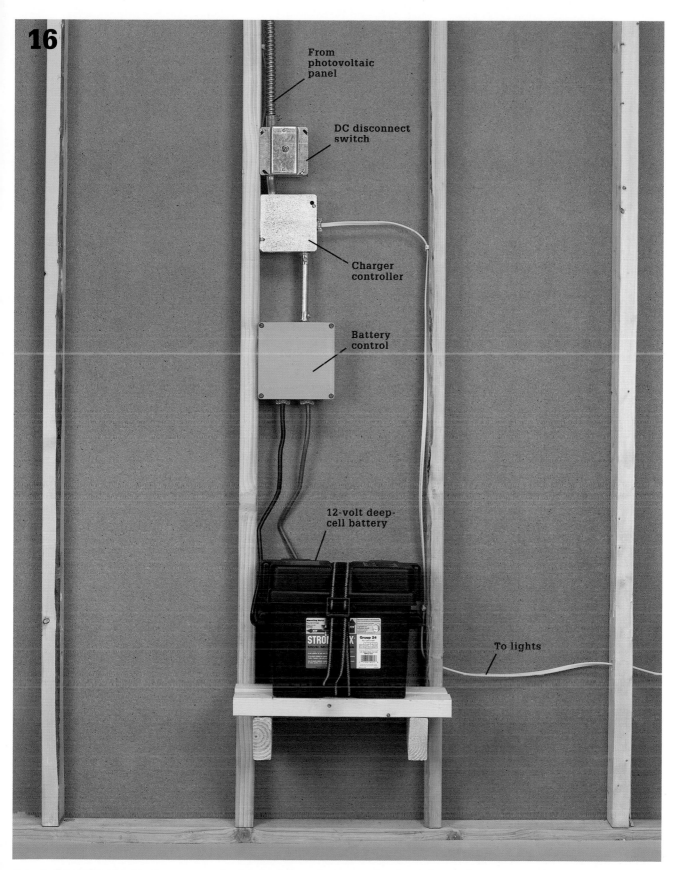

From photovoltaic panel

DC disconnect switch

Charger controller

Battery control

12-volt deep-cell battery

To lights

Cover all junction boxes, then remove the bag from the collector panel and turn the DC disconnect switch on to complete the circuit. Test the lights and adjust the time to desired setting.

Backup Power Supply

Installing a backup generator is an invaluable way to prepare your family for emergencies. The simplest backup power system is a portable gas-powered generator and an extension cord or two. A big benefit of this approach is that you can run a refrigerator and a few worklights during a power outage with a tool that can also be transported to remote job sites or on camping trips when it's not doing emergency backup duty. This is also the least expensive way to provide some backup power for your home. You can purchase a generator at most home centers and be up and running in a matter of hours. If you take this approach, it is critically important that you make certain any loads being run by your generator are disconnected from the utility power source.

The next step up is to incorporate a manual transfer switch for your portable generator. Transfer switches are permanently hardwired to your service panel. They are mounted on either the interior or the exterior of your house between the generator and the service panel. You provide a power feed from the generator into the switch. The switch is wired to selected essential circuits in your house, allowing you to power lights, furnace blowers, and other loads that can't easily be run with an extension cord. But perhaps the most important job a transfer switch performs is to disconnect the utility power. If the inactive utility power line is attached to the service panel, "backfeed" of power from your generator to the utility line can occur when the generator kicks in. This condition could be fatal to line workers who are trying to restore power. The potential for backfeed is the main reason many municipalities insist that only a licensed electrician hook up a transfer switch. Using a transfer switch not installed by a professional may also void the warranty of the switch and the generator.

Automatic transfer switches turn on the generator and switch off the utility supply when they detect a significant drop in line voltage. They may be installed with portable generators, provided the generator is equipped with an electric starter.

Large standby generators that resemble central air conditioners are the top of the line in backup power supply systems. Often fueled by home natural gas lines or propane tanks that offer a bottomless fuel source, standby generators are made in sizes with as much as 20 to 40 kilowatts of output—enough to supply all of the power needs of a 5,000-sq.-ft. home.

Generators have a range of uses.
Large hard-wired models can provide instant emergency power for a whole house. Smaller models (below) are convenient for occasional short-term backup as well as job sites or camping trips.

Choosing a Backup Generator

A 2,000- to 5,000-watt gas-powered generator and a few extension cords can power lamps and an appliance or two during shorter-term power outages. Appliances must not be connected to household wiring and the generator simultaneously. Never plug a generator into an outlet. Never operate a generator indoors. Run extension cords through a garage door.

A permanent transfer switch patches electricity from a large portable generator through to selected household circuits via an inlet at your service panel (inset), allowing you to power hardwired fixtures and appliances with the generator.

For full, on-demand backup service, install a large standby generator wired through to an automatic transfer panel. In the event of a power outage, the household system instantly switches to the generator.

A Typical Backup System

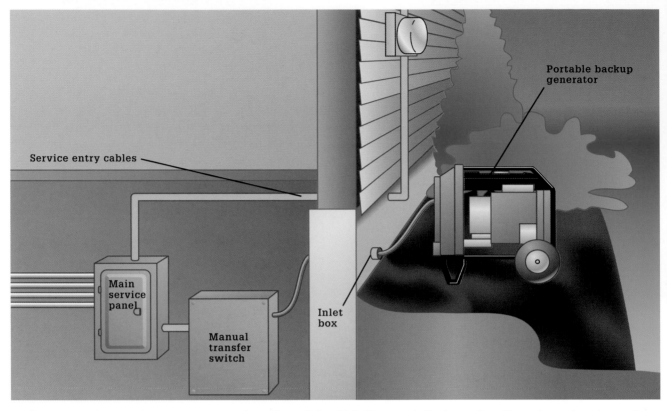

Service entry cables

Portable backup generator

Main service panel

Manual transfer switch

Inlet box

Backup generators supply power to a manual transfer switch, which disconnects the house from the main service wires and routes power from the generator through selected household circuits.

Choosing a Generator

Choosing a generator for your home's needs requires a few calculations. The chart below gives an estimate of the size of generator typically recommended for a house of a certain size. You can get a more accurate number by adding up the power consumption (the watts) of all the circuits or devices to be powered by a generator. It's also important to keep in mind that, for most electrical appliances, the amount of power required at the moment you flip the ON switch is greater than the number of watts required to keep the device running. For instance, though an air conditioner may run on 15,000 watts of power, it will require a surge of 30,000 watts at startup (the power range required to operate an appliance is usually listed somewhere on the device itself). These two numbers are called run watts and surge watts. Generators are typically sold according to run watts (a 5,000-watt generator can sustain 5,000 watts). They are also rated for a certain number of surge watts (a 5,000-watt generator may be able to produce

a surge of 10,000 watts). If the surge watts aren't listed, ask or check the manual. Some generators can't develop many more surge watts than run watts; others can produce twice as much surge as run wattage.

It's not necessary to buy a generator large enough to match the surge potential of all your circuits (you won't be turning everything on simultaneously), but surge watts should factor in your purchasing decision. If you will be operating the generator at or near capacity, it is also a wise practice to stagger startups for appliances.

SIZE OF HOUSE (IN SQUARE FEET)	RECOMMENDED GENERATOR SIZE (IN KILOWATTS)
Up to 2,700	5–11
2,700–3,700	14–16
3,700–4,700	20
4,700–7,000	42–47

Cord-connected Transfer Switches

Cord-connected transfer switches (shown above) are hard-wired to the service panel (in some cases they're installed after the service panel and operate only selected circuits). These switches contain a male receptacle for a power supply cord connected to the generator. Automatic transfer switches (not shown) detect voltage drop-off in the main power line and switch over to the emergency power source.

When using a cord-connected switch, consider mounting an inlet box to the exterior wall. This will allow you to connect a generator without running a cord into the house.

Generator Tips ▶

If you'll need to run sensitive electronics such as computers or home theater equipment, look for a generator with power inverter technology that dispenses "clean power" with a stable sine wave pattern.

A generator that will output 240-volt service is required to run most central air conditioners. If your generator has variable output (120/240), make sure the switch is set to the correct output voltage.

Running & Maintaining a Backup System

Even with a fully automatic standby generator system fueled by natural gas or propane, you will need to conduct some regular maintenance and testing to make sure all systems are ready in the event of power loss. If you're depending on a portable generator and extension cords or a standby generator with a manual transfer switch, you'll also need to know the correct sequence of steps to follow in a power emergency. Switches and panels also need to be tested on a regular basis, as directed in your owner's manual. And be sure that all switches (both interior and exterior) are housed in an approved enclosure box.

Pull-cord starter

Smaller portable generators often use pull-cords instead of electric starters.

ANATOMY OF A PORTABLE BACKUP GENERATOR

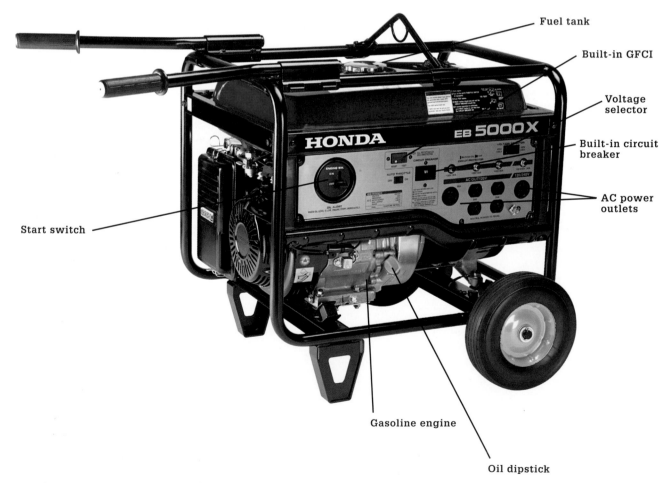

Fuel tank

Built-in GFCI

Voltage selector

Built-in circuit breaker

AC power outlets

Start switch

Gasoline engine

Oil dipstick

Portable generators use small gasoline engines to generate power. A built-in electronics panel sets current to AC or DC and the correct voltage. Most models will also include a built-in circuit breaker to protect the generator from damage in the event it is connected to too many loads. Better models include features like built-in GFCI protection. Larger portable generators may also feature electric starter motors and batteries for push-button starts.

Operating a Manual System During an Outage

Plug the generator in at the inlet box. Make sure the other end of the generator's outlet cord is plugged into the appropriate outlet on the generator (120-volt or 120/240-volt AC) and the generator is switched to the appropriate voltage setting.

Start the generator with the pull-cord or electric starter (if your generator has one). Let the generator run for several minutes before flipping the transfer switch.

Flip the manual transfer switch. Begin turning on loads one at a time by flipping breakers on, starting with the ones that power essential equipment. Do not overload the generator or the switch and do not run the generator at or near full capacity for more than 30 minutes at a time.

Maintaining and Operating an Automatic Standby Generator

If you choose to spend the money and install a dedicated standby generator of 10,000 watts or more and operate it through an automatic transfer switch or panel, you won't need to lift a hand when your utility power goes out. The system kicks in by itself. However, you should follow the manufacturer's suggestions for testing the system, changing the oil, and running the motor periodically.

Installing a Transfer Switch

A transfer switch is installed next to the main service panel to override the normal electrical service with power from a backup generator during a power outage. Manual transfer switches require an operator to change the power source, while automatic switches detect the loss of power, start the back-up generator and switch over to the backup power feed. Because the amount of electricity created by a backup generator is not adequate to power all of the electrical circuits in your house, you'll need to designate a few selected circuits to get backup current (See Sidebar).

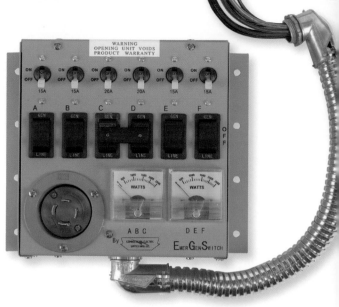

A manual transfer switch connects emergency circuits in your main panel to a standby generator.

Tools & Materials ▸

Circuit tester
Drill/driver
Screwdrivers
Hammer
Wire cutters
Cable ripper
Wire strippers

Level
Manual transfer switch
Screws
Wire connectors
  (yellow)
Standby power
  generator

One flip of a switch reassigns the power source for each critical circuit so your backup generator can keep your refrigerator, freezer and important lights running during an outage of utility power.

Selecting Backup Circuits ▸

Before you purchase a backup generator, determine which loads you will want to power from your generator in the event of a power loss. Generally, you will want to power your refrigerator, freezer, and maybe a few lights. Add up the running wattage ratings of the appliances you will power up to determine how large your backup generator needs to be. Because the startup wattage of many appliances is higher than the running wattage, avoid starting all circuits at the same time—it can cause an overload situation with your generator. Here are some approximate running wattage guidelines.

- Refrigerator: 750 watts
- Forced air furnace: 1100 to 1500 watts.

- Incandescent lights: 60 watts per bulb (CFL and LED lights use less wattage)
- Sump pump: 800 to 1000 watts
- Garage door opener: 550 to 1100 watts
- Television: 300 watts

Add the wattage values of all the loads you want to power and multiply the sum by 1.25. This will give you the minimum wattage your generator must produce. Portable standby generators typically output 5,000 to 7,500 watts. Most larger, stationary generator can output 10,000 to 20,000 watts (10 to 20 kilowatts).

How to Install a Manual Transfer Switch

1

Turn off the main power breaker in your electrical service panel. CAUTION: The terminals where power enters the main breakers will still be energized.

2

Determine which household circuits are critical for emergency usage during a power outage. Typically, this will include the refrigerator, freezer, furnace, and at least one light or small appliance circuit.

(continued)

3

Match your critical circuits with circuit inlet on your pre-wired transfer switch. Try to balance the load as best you can: for example, if your refrigerator is on the leftmost circuit, connect your freezer to the circuit farthest to the right. Double-pole (240-volt) circuits will require two 120-volt circuit connections. Also make sure that 15-amp and 20-amp circuits are not mismatched with one another.

4

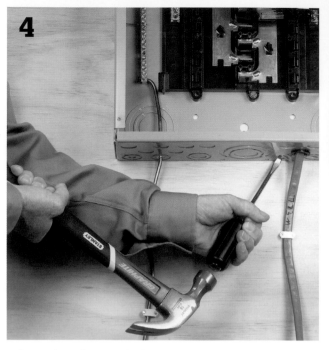

Select a knockout at the bottom of the main service panel box and remove the knockout. Make sure to choose a knockout that is sized to match the connector on the flexible conduit coming from the transfer switch.

5

Feed the wires from the transfer switch into the knock out hole, taking care not to damage the insulation. You will note that each wire is labeled according to which circuit in the switch box it feeds.

6

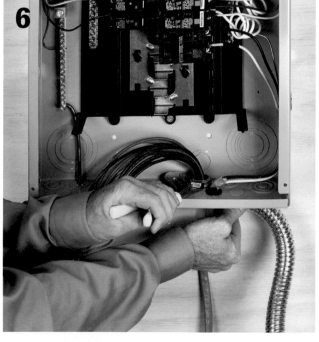

Secure the flexible conduit from the switch box to the main service panel using a locknut and a bushing where required.

Attach the transfer switch box to the wall so the closer edge is about 18" away from the center of the main service panel. Use whichever connectors make sense for your wall type.

Remove the breaker for the first critical circuit from the main service panel box and disconnect the hot wire lead from the lug on the breaker.

Locate the red wire for the switch box circuit that corresponds to the circuit you've disconnected. Attach the red wire to the breaker you've just removed and then reinstall the breaker.

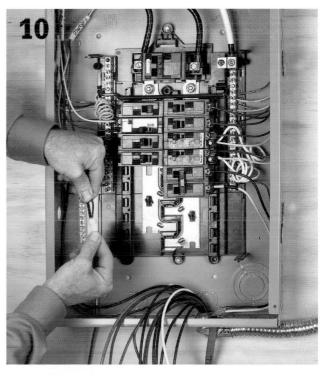

Locate the black wire from the same transfer switch circuit and twist it together with the old feed wire, using a yellow wire connector. Tuck the wires neatly out of the way at the edges of the box. Proceed to the next circuit and repeat the process.

(continued)

If any of your critical circuits are 240-volt circuits, attach the red leads from the two transfer switch circuits to the double-pole breaker. The two circuits originating in the transfer switch should be next to one another and their switches should be connected with a handle tie. If you have no 240-volt circuits you may remove the preattached handle tie and use the circuits individually.

Once you have made all circuit connections, attach the white neutral wire from the transfer switch to an opening in the neutral bus bar of the main service panel.

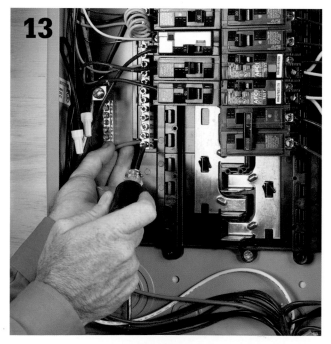

Attach the green ground wire from the transfer switch to an open port on the grounding bar in your main service panel. This should complete the installation of the transfer switch. Replace the cover on the service panel box and make sure to fill in the circuit map on your switch box.

Begin testing the transfer switch by making sure all of the switches on the transfer switch box are set to the LINE setting. The power should still be OFF at the main panel breakers.

Make sure your standby generator is operating properly and has been installed professionally. See page 83 for information on choosing a generator that is sized appropriately for your needs.

15

Before turning your generator on, attach the power cord from the generator to the switch box. Never attach or detach a generator cord with the generator running. Turn your standby power generator on and let it run for a minute or two.

16

Flip each circuit switch on the transfer switch box to GEN, one at a time. Try to maintain balance by moving back and forth from circuits on the left and right side. Do not turn all circuits on at the same time. Observe the onboard wattage meters as you engage each circuit and try to keep the wattage levels in balance. When you have completed testing the switch, turn the switches back to LINE and then shut off your generator.

A digital autoranging multimeter is the primary diagnostic tool for troubleshooting most home wiring systems and fixtures. Here, the multimeter is indicating a voltage drop outside the normal range.

Troubleshooting & Repairs

Running new circuits and hooking up new fixtures are fairly predictable projects when it comes to estimating time and expense. This is less true with repairing problems in your system and fixtures. In some cases, a repair is as simple as opening an electrical box, spotting a loose wire connector and remaking the connection. But there are also times when fixing a dead circuit or device is a highly frustrating proposition. Such cases are almost always caused by tricky diagnostic challenges. Wires are hidden behind walls and there very often are no visual clues to system breakdowns. So essentially, minimizing repair frustration boils down to learning to deploy logical, systematic diagnostics. Educated troubleshooting, you could say.

In this project you'll learn how to use the most important diagnostic tool in any electrician's toolkit: the multimeter. These handy devices come in a dizzying array of types and qualities, but for diagnostic purposes they are used to take readings for current (amperage), voltage and continuity (whether an electrical path is open or closed). Once you learn the basics of operating a multimeter, you can enlist it in a logical, deductive manner to track down the source of a wiring problem. Once located, correcting the problem is usually very simple.

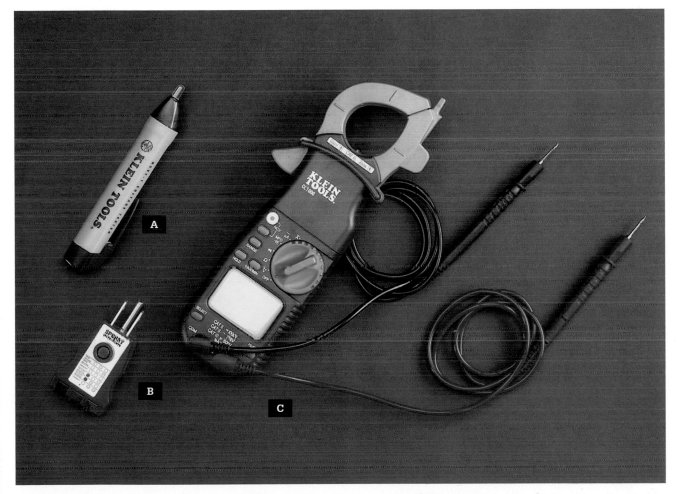

Diagnostic tools for home wiring use include: Touchless circuit tester (A) to safely check wires for current and confirm that circuits are dead; Plug-in tester (B) to check receptacles for correct polarity, grounding and circuit protection; Multimeter (C) to measure AC/DC voltage, AC/DC current, resistance, capacitance, frequency and duty cycle (model shown is an auto-ranging digital multimeter with clamp-on jaws that measure through sheathing and wire insulation).

Multimeters

Multimeters are nearly indispensible diagnostic tools for doing intermediate to advanced level electrical work (as well as automotive and electronics repair). They are used to measure voltage, current (amperage) and a few other conditions such as continuity, capacitance and frequency. For your home electrical system, by far the most used feature of a multimeter is testing voltage and current, although there are occasions where testing for resistance is needed. Among professional electricians, the most common and widely used multimeters have a clamp-on ammeter that measures current through the wire insulation so you don't have to disconnect the circuit and expose bare wire. Most clamp-on multimeters also are fitted with insertible probes with which you can measure voltage and continuity in the traditional way. An example of a clamp-on multimeter can be seen on the next page. Among homeowners, however, the most common multimeters these days are digital, auto-ranging tools that use probes or alligator clamps at the ends of wire leads for diagnostic work. Older multimeters that do not have autoranging capability must be pre-set to estimated calibration levels before use. Non-digital multimeters or ammeters usually have a dial gauge that gives readouts. These tools are somewhat more difficult to use and are less precise. Considering that digital, autoranging multimeters can be found for just a few dollars (the top of the line models cost over $100) there is really no good reason not to replace your old device with one that resembles the tools seen on these pages.

Time to Replace that Neon Tester ▶

Neon circuit testers are inexpensive and easy to use (if the light glows the circuit is hot), but they are less sensitive than multimeters and can be unsafe. In some cases, neon testers won't detect the presence of lower voltage in a circuit. This can lead you to believe that a circuit is shut off when it is not—a dangerous mistake. The small probes on a neon circuit tester also force you to get too close to live terminals and wires. For the most reliable readings, buy and learn to use a multimeter. At the very least, switch to a touchless tester like the one on page 101, Step 1.

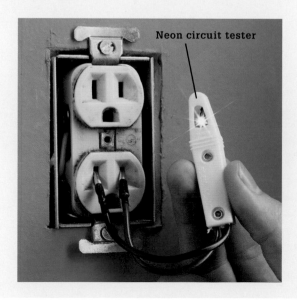

Neon circuit tester

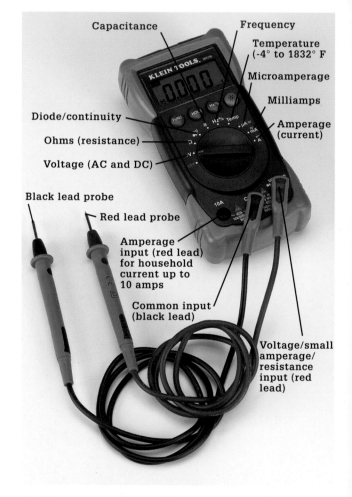

Capacitance

Frequency

Temperature (-4° to 1832° F

Microamperage

Milliamps

Diode/continuity

Amperage (current)

Ohms (resistance)

Voltage (AC and DC)

Black lead probe

Red lead probe

Amperage input (red lead) for household current up to 10 amps

Common input (black lead)

Voltage/small amperage/resistance input (red lead)

A digital, autoranging multimeter must be adjusted to the proper setting for the reading you want to take. The probe leads also must be inserted into the correct inlet at the bottom of the tool. Inserting the red lead into the incorrect inlet can cause the tool to trip an internal fuse. Study your owner's manual carefully before using any tool.

How to Measure Current

1

Create access to the wires you need to test. In most cases this requires that you remove the cover to an electrical service panel or an electrical box (inset).

2

Set the multimeter to test for amperage (current is measured in amperes or amps). On some multimeters you need to select between amperage settings that are above or below 40 amps. Use the rated amperage of the circuit as a guide (amperage is printed on the circuit breaker switch).

3

Clamp the jaws of a clamp-on multimeter onto the conductor or one of the conductors (if more than one) leading to a circuit breaker. If you are using a non-clamping multimeter, touch one probe to the screw terminal where the hot lead is attached to the breaker and touch the other probe to the metal panel box. The readout on your meter is the amount of current flowing in that circuit.

Taking Measurements at a Receptacle ▸

You may use a multimeter to measure for voltage at a wall receptacle. Regardless of whether the outlet is in service, if it is live you will get a voltage reading in the approximate range of the receptacle rating—here, 120 volts. To detect live current, measured in amps, the receptacle must be in use, with an appliance drawing from it. Taking an amperage reading in such an instance will only yield the amount of current being drawn, which is a factor of the appliance, not the circuit capacity.

How to Measure Voltage

1

2

3

To measure voltage using the multimeter, you will have to use the two probes provided with the multimeter and have access to a live terminal or slot as well as a grounded terminal or slot. If your meter has probe holders at the top, snap the probes into them. They are like extra hands.

Turn the multimeter to the VAC setting to measure AC voltage that is found in your house. Set the multimeter to VDC if measuring DC voltage, such as in a car or a battery-fed device. On some multimeters, like the one above, you select "V" for voltage then change between AC and DC with the "FUNC" button.

To measure the AC voltage, place one probe on a grounded surface, such as the metallic junction box or the bare ground wire. Place the other probe on the hot screw terminal or into the receptacle slot associated with the hot wire. The voltage readout should be in the range of 120 volts, plus or minus 5 volts (usually 120 volts in a residence in the US).

240 VOLTS. You can also measure voltage across the two hot leads to determine if you have 240 volts. This can be done at your range receptacle, dryer receptacle, or any other 240-volt receptacle. Place one probe in one of the small slots and the other probe in the other slot directly across from it. The voltage should read 240 volts, plus or minus 5 volts.

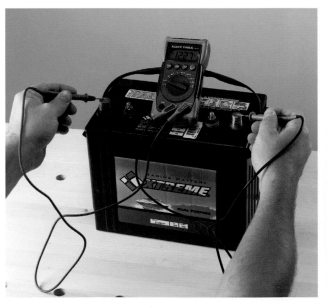

DC Voltage. When testing DC voltage, such as in a car battery, you can measure exactly the same way as for AC as long as the meter is set to the DC function. For more accurate results, test the voltage while the battery is in use.

How to Test for Continuity

Continuity is a condition in a circuit where the conductors form an unbroken pathway through which current may flow. When measuring for continuity, always make sure there is no power present on the circuit you are testing or damage may occur to the meter. You can also measure the resistance in this mode as well.

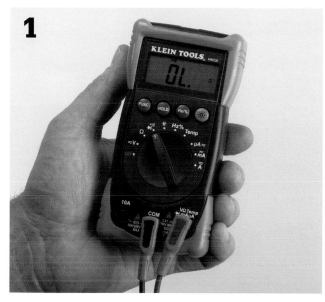

The setting for continuity is an "audible" or diode symbol display on the dial. Select this setting

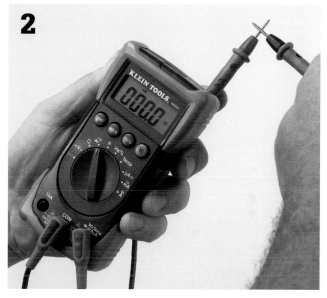

Verify that the continuity tester is functional by touching the two probes together. You should hear an alert sound and/or see a reading of zero ohms (Ohms is a value of the resistance to current flow).

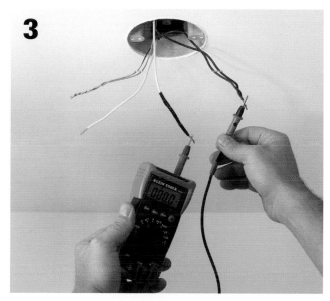

To test a circuit, touch one probe to one of the wires on a given circuit and the other to the second wire of the circuit. If you hear an audible sound or read a value of resistance other than zero, you have a complete or unbroken path for current to flow.

How to Test a 3-way Switch ▶

Remove the switch from the circuit and place one of the probes onto the common terminal and the other probe onto one of the other two terminals used for the traveler wires. If the meter indicates infinity ohms or there is no sound, flip the switch and if it is in working order the meter should read zero ohms or emit an audible sound. It should only work in one direction or the other, not both.

Troubleshooting an Open Neutral

An open neutral is an electrical problem where the circuit is broken on the return path wire or neutral (white wire). When this situation occurs anything plugged into or connected to this circuit can experience low or high voltage, which could damage voltage sensitive electronics such as a computer or flat screen TV. The lights will be dim or not work at all, depending upon where the problem lies within the circuit.

Possible Symptoms of an Open Neutral ›

1. When a whole circuit does not work and the breaker associated with that circuit is operating normally.
2. When the neutral or white wire registers as a hot wire by using a non contact voltage tester when the circuit breaker is on. This most likely indicates a problem between the main service panel and the utility transformer. The condition should be readable on other receptacles as well.
3. If you register a voltage lower than 110 volts between the hot and neutral.
4. When the incandescent lights work, but are very dim.
5. When the fluorescent lights are barely lit and are flickering.
6. Discoloration of the wires or exposed copper turning green under the wirenut holding the neutral wires together.

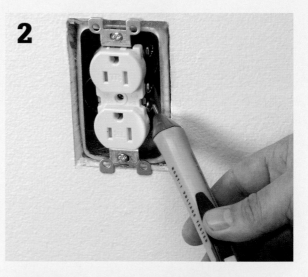

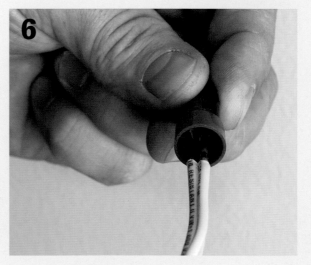

How to Troubleshoot an Open Neutral

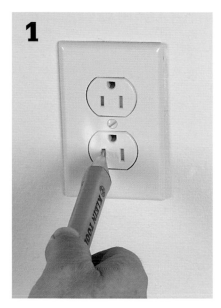

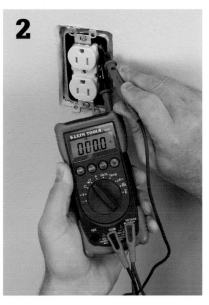

Verify which lights and receptacles are on the circuit by turning the breaker off and by checking for power with a non-contact voltage tester. It is helpful to either draw a map of the house or place some tape on every affected opening.

Start at the outlet nearest to the panel. With the breaker off and using a multimeter, check for continuity between the neutral (white wire) and the ground (bare or green wire). These two wires land at the same point electrically in your electrical panel. If there is an indication of continuity between these two wires, the neutral and ground connections are sound and you should proceed to the next outlet as you move away from the panel.

When you encounter a point at which you read infinity ohms or there is no continuity between the neutral and ground wires, the problem lies within the connections in that box or the box just upstream (toward) the panel from the one you are checking. Sometimes you will see evidence of arcing on the wire cap containing the connection which may include discoloration, or a blackish char near the copper.

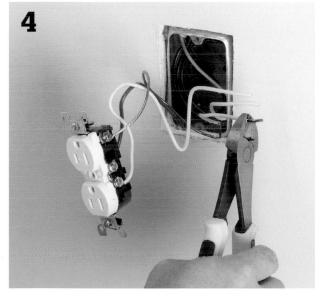

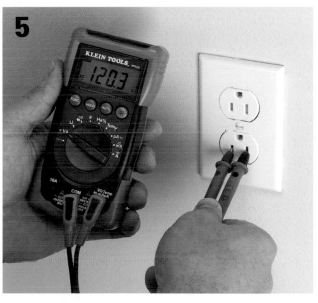

When you have found the problem connection, remove the wire cap and, if it is possible, cut the damaged portions of the wires off and restrip the wires to expose new copper. Line the wire ends up and twist on a new wire cap.

Turn the circuit breaker back on and verify the proper voltage is present at your receptacles by measuring with a multimeter.

Troubleshooting a Short Circuit

Short circuits are a direct connection between the hot or power wire (black or red) and to either the neutral (white) or ground (bare) wire. This connection between the two will cause your circuit breaker or fuse to blow, which should interrupt power to the affected circuit.

Short circuits are a common problem and can usually be solved by taking the following steps. The idea behind electrical troubleshooting is to simplify the circuit by checking it at certain points, in order to narrow down the problem point by process of elimination. Generally, the problem is that there is a bare ground wire touching a hot terminal within a switch or an outlet box. There will usually be a black scorched mark or some sign of an electrical arc where the problem lies.

How to Troubleshoot a Short Circuit

1

2

Turn the power off at the affected breaker and verify with a non-contact voltage tester that there is no power present. Unplug everything from the receptacles and turn the lights off on the circuit that is affected.

Using a multimeter set to the ohms or continuity setting, check the wires at the panel. Touch one of the probes to the hot or black wire and the other probe to the ground or bare wire. If the meter rings or indicates a low resistance value, you have a direct short to ground. If the meter does not ring or indicates a high resistance value the circuit is clear. If the meter does not ring, start by turning the switches on one-by-one and re-testing to verify the resistance value. If the meter indicates a low resistance value or a short circuit, the problem is downstream from the switch or within the light fixture itself.

3

If the meter consistently rings or indicates a low resistive value, you will need to find the electrical box that contains the affected circuit. Choose a box that is convenient to open and preferably in the middle of the run, such as a receptacle. Verify there is no power present by touching all of the wires within the box with a non-contact voltage tester.

4

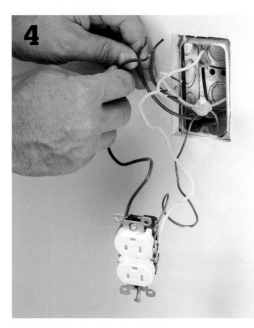

If the box you have chosen is in fact in the middle of the run, it will contain at least two cables. Remove the receptacle from the two cables and separate all of the wires.

5

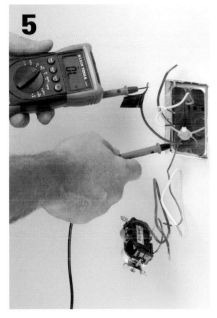

Check the resistance between the black and the ground on both sets of cables. One of the cables should cause the continuity alert to ring and the other should not. Mark the affected one with a piece of black tape and place wire caps over the exposed ends of the black wires.

6

Check the wires at the panel to see if the short has cleared. If the short is clear, the problem lies down stream from the opened box and it is now safe to turn the breaker back on to help eliminate further problem points. If the short is still present, the problem lies between the opened electrical box and the panel.

7

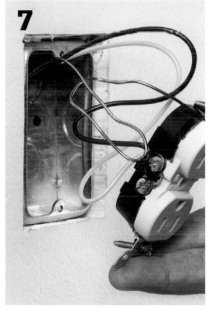

Choose another box in the middle of the affected circuit, there by narrowing down the possible problem areas until the short circuit can be positively identified and corrected. When you have discovered the short circuit, verify the wires are still in good shape and repair the connection.

Common Residential Wiring Codes

Home wiring is a very popular do-it-yourself subject that is fundamentally hazardous. When it comes to electricity, mistakes and accidents do pose threats including fire, injury, and death. Therefore, safety is the primary focus of the electrical code provisions.

In this chapter you will find many of the rules governing safe installation of electrical wires, electrical equipment—including conduit, electrical receptacles, switches, lights, and other fixtures. Use this information to inspect your wiring and make sure it all conforms to code. If it does not, or if you are unsure about it, have a professional electrician upgrade your electrical system.

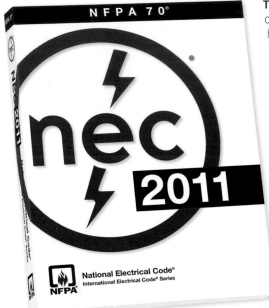

The National Electrical Code (NEC), and local electrical codes and building codes, provide guidelines for determining how much power and how many circuits your home needs. Your local electrical inspector can tell you which regulations apply to your job.

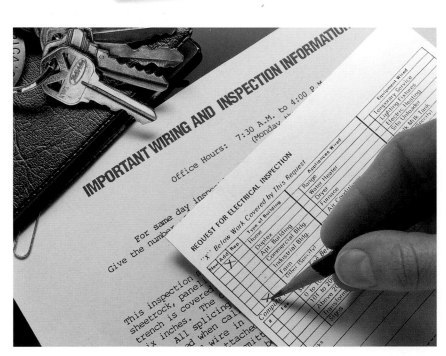

Prepare for inspections. Remember that your work must be reviewed by your local electrical inspector. When planning your wiring project, always follow the inspector's guidelines for quality workmanship.

General Requirements

CLOSURE OF UNUSED OPENINGS

1. Close all openings in boxes, conduit bodies, and cabinets with material that provides protection equal to the original opening cover. This means using plastic or metal knockout covers. Tape and cardboard do not provide equal protection.
2. Recess metal knockout covers in nonmetallic boxes and conduit bodies at least ¼ inch from the surface of the box or conduit body.
3. Cover open outlet boxes with a blank cover, a blank plate, or fixture canopy. Switch plates and receptacle plates do not provide complete closure for electrical boxes.
4. Ground metal covers and plates.

IDENTIFICATION OF CIRCUITS IN ELECTRICAL PANELS

1. Provide a legible and permanent marking or label that identifies the purpose of circuit breakers, fuses, and other equipment used to disconnect power from a circuit. Identify the circuit in enough detail so that it can be distinguished from all other circuits. Example: do not identify a circuit as general lighting. Identify the specific rooms or outlets served by the circuit. A marking or label is not required if the purpose of the disconnecting equipment is self-evident. Use marking or labeling materials that will withstand the environment where the disconnecting equipment is located.
2. Locate the circuit identification on the face of the panelboard enclosure or on the inside panelboard door.

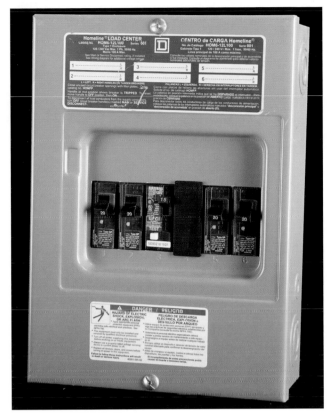

Cover open circuit breaker knockouts with an approved plastic or metal cover.

PROHIBITED LOCATIONS FOR EXISTING ELECTRICAL PANELS

1. Do not locate electrical panels and circuit breakers or fuses in clothes closets, bathrooms, or spaces designated for storage.

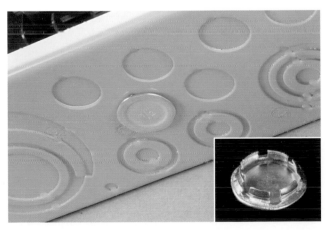

Cover open conduit knockouts in electrical boxes with an approved plastic or metal cap (inset).

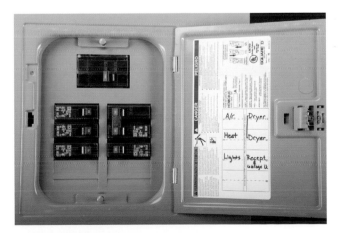

Label each circuit in all electrical panels so that the purpose of each circuit is clear.

WORKING CLEARANCES AROUND ELECTRICAL PANELS

1. Inspect your electrical service panel to make sure it conforms to code. If not, hire a professional electrician to relocate it. Panel should have a clear working space in front of electrical panel enclosures and other equipment and enclosures that require access while interior parts are energized. Examples of other enclosures and equipment include air conditioner and furnace service-disconnect boxes.

2. Clear working space should be at least 36 inches deep, and at least 30 inches wide (or as wide as the enclosure, if it is wider than 30 inches), and at least 78 inches high. Measure the clear working space in front of the enclosure beginning at the front of the enclosure. Measure the clear working space from the energized parts, if the parts requiring access are not in an enclosure.

3. Panel should have enough clearance so that the enclosure door can be opened at least 90 degrees.

4. Do not allow any objects located above or below the electrical enclosures to extend into the clear working space more than six inches beyond the front of the electrical enclosure.

5. Panel should provide access to the clear working space. Do not block access with shelves, workbenches, or other difficult to move objects.

CLEAR SPACE ABOVE & BELOW ELECTRICAL PANEL ENCLOSURES

1. Maintain a clear space directly above and below electrical panel enclosures, free from any components not associated with the electrical system. This space is intended for wires entering and leaving the electrical panel. Do not install plumbing pipes, HVAC ducts, and similar components in this space.

2. Maintain a clear space that is at least the width and depth of the electrical panel enclosure.

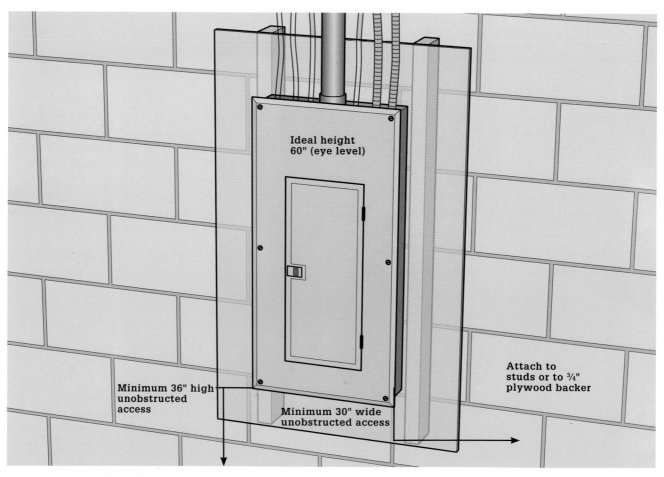

Ideal height 60" (eye level)

Attach to studs or to ¾" plywood backer

Minimum 36" high unobstructed access

Minimum 30" wide unobstructed access

Your equipment should include a safe space above, in front of, and below all electrical panels and similar electrical equipment. If your panel does not meet these standards, have it relocated by a professional.

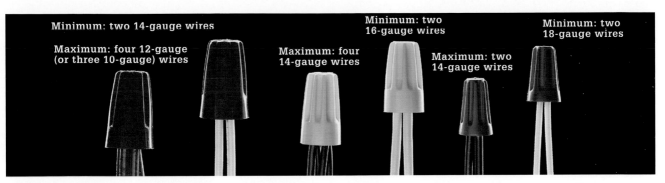

Minimum: two 14-gauge wires

Maximum: four 12-gauge
(or three 10-gauge) wires

Maximum: four
14-gauge wires

Minimum: two
16-gauge wires

Maximum: two
14-gauge wires

Minimum: two
18-gauge wires

Use wire connectors rated for the wires you are connecting. Wire connectors are color-coded by size, but the coding scheme varies according to manufacturer. The wire connectors shown above come from one major manufacturer. To ensure safe connections, each connector is rated for both minimum and maximum wire capacity. These connectors can be used to connect both conducting wires and grounding wires. Green wire connectors are used only for grounding wires.

SPLICING WIRES

1. Splice (join) wires using only listed devices such as appropriate sized wire connectors. Use wire connector according to manufacturer's recommendations regarding the minimum and maximum number and size of wires that the connector can accommodate.
2. Cover spliced wires with material equal to the original insulation. This does not include electrical tape or similar materials.
3. For splice wires that will be buried in the ground, use only devices listed for direct burial and install them according to manufacturer's instructions.
4. Provide access to spliced wires, unless the splice and splicing device are specifically allowed to be concealed. Access is usually provided by an accessible, covered junction box.
5. Do not place wire splices in a raceway unless the raceway has a removable cover.

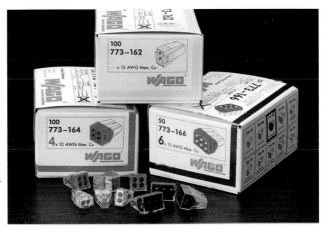

Push-in connectors are a relatively new product for joining wires. Instead of twisting the bare wire ends together, you strip off about ¾" of insulation and insert them into a hole in the connector. The connectors come with two to four holes sized for various gauge wires. These connectors are perfect for inexperienced DIYers because they do not pull apart like a sloppy twisted connection can.

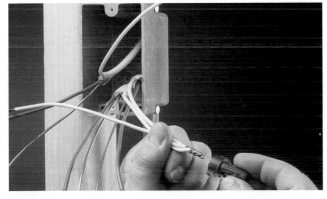

Twist wire connectors over the ends of individual conductors that have been stripped of insulation. Pre-twist wires together with pliers or linesmans' pliers (optional). Do not leave bare wire exposed beneath bottom of connector.

SPLICING ALUMINUM & COPPER WIRES

1. Splice (join) aluminum and copper wires together using devices listed for splicing aluminum and copper wires. Look for a mark or label such as AL/CU on the device or on the package for assurance that the device is listed for splicing aluminum and copper wires. Some wire nuts sold for residential use are not listed for splicing aluminum and copper wires.
2. Use only inhibitors and antioxidant compounds that are approved for splicing aluminum and copper wires. These materials should not degrade or damage the wires, wire insulation, or equipment. Read and follow manufacturer's instructions.

LENGTH OF WIRES EXTENDING FROM BOXES

1. Extend wires at least three inches beyond the opening of any electrical box, junction, or switch point, if the opening is less than eight inches in any direction. This applies to most switch, receptacle, and light fixture mounting boxes used in residential electrical systems.

2. Extend wires at least six inches beyond where the wires emerge from the raceway or cable sheathing. Example: NM cable enters a single residential switch box with one inch of intact sheathing (outer cover). Begin the six inches measurement where the sheathing ends. The cable should extend at least seven inches from the rear of the box. The NM cable should also extend at least three inches beyond the outside edge of the box.

CONNECTING WIRES TO TERMINALS

1. Remove insulation from wires and connect wires to terminals without damaging the wire. Do not connect damaged wires to terminals. Example: if you nick, damage, or cut strands from a stranded wire, cut the wire back to where it is full size and use the full, undamaged wire.

2. Connect more than one wire to a terminal only if the terminal is identified to accept multiple wires. Example: many panelboards require one wire per terminal for the grounded (neutral)

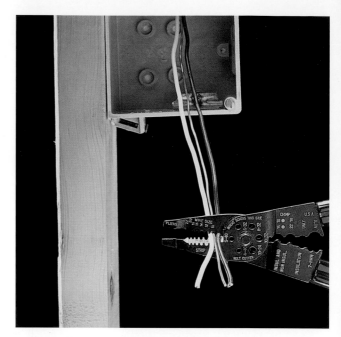

Extend wires past the box opening at least 3".

wires and allow two or more same gauge wires per terminal for the equipment grounding wires. Example: many circuit breakers allow only one hot (ungrounded) wire per circuit breaker terminal.

3. Connect aluminum wires to terminals only if the terminal is identified to accept aluminum wires.

VIOLATION! Do not connect multiple neutral or hot wires to a terminal unless specifically allowed (neutral bus bar seen here has two neutral conductors connected to single terminal).

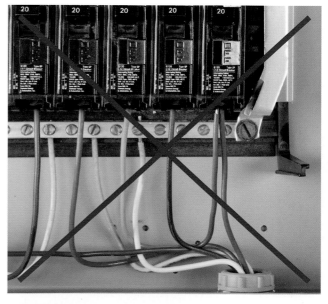

VIOLATION! Never connect multiple hot wires to the same terminal on circuit breakers or other electrical devices unless specifically allowed by the manufacturer.

WIRE COLOR CODES

1. Use wires with white or gray colored insulation or wires with three white stripes on other than green insulation as neutral (grounded) wires. You may use wires with other than white or gray colored insulation as neutral (grounded) wires if they are larger than #6 AWG and if you mark them with a permanent white marking at all wire terminations.

2. Use wires with green colored insulation or wires with green colored insulation and at least one yellow stripe as equipment grounding wires. You may use uninsulated (bare) wires as equipment grounding wires in most circuits.

3. You may use any color other than white, gray, or green as hot (ungrounded) wires. The common colors are red and black. You may use a wire with white or gray insulation as a hot (ungrounded) wire if the wire is part of a cable (such as NM) and if you permanently mark it as a hot (ungrounded) conductor at all places where the wire is visible and accessible. This marking is usually done by wrapping the end of the wire with black or red electrical tape.

NEUTRAL & EQUIPMENT GROUNDING WIRE CONTINUITY

1. Connect neutral (grounded) wires together in device boxes if the neutral (grounded) wire is part of a multiwire branch circuit. Do not rely on any device, such as a receptacle or light fixture, to provide the connection for the neutral (grounded) wire in a multiwire branch circuit.

2. Connect equipment grounding wires together in all device boxes. Do not rely on any device, such as a receptacle or light fixture, to provide the connection for the equipment grounding wire in any circuit.

3. Install a wire (called a pigtail) between the connected wires and any device in the box.

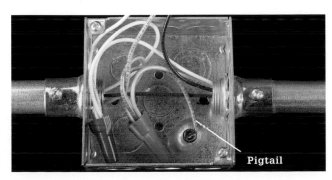

Use a pigtail when you need to connect multiple wires together and use one wire to connect to a terminal.

Wire Color Chart ▸

WIRE COLOR		FUNCTION
	White	neutral wire: at zero voltage in many, but not all, circuits
	Black	hot wire carrying current at full voltage
	Red	hot wire carrying current at full voltage
	White, Black markings	hot wire carrying current at full voltage
	Green	serves as a grounding pathway
	Bare copper	serves as a grounding pathway

Individual wires are color-coded to identify their function. In some circuit installations, the white wire serves as a hot wire that carries voltage. If so, this white wire may be labeled with black tape or paint to identify it as a hot wire.

Wire Size Chart ▸

WIRE GAUGE		WIRE CAPACITY & USE
	#6	55 amps; central air conditioner, electric furnace
	#8	40 amps; electric range, central air conditioner
	#10	30 amps; window air conditioner, clothes dryer
	#12	20 amps; light fixtures, receptacles, microwave oven
	#14	15 amps; light fixtures, receptacles
	#16	light-duty extension cords
	#18 to 22	thermostats, doorbells, security systems

Wire sizes (shown actual size) are categorized by the American Wire Gauge system. The larger the wire size, the smaller the AWG number.

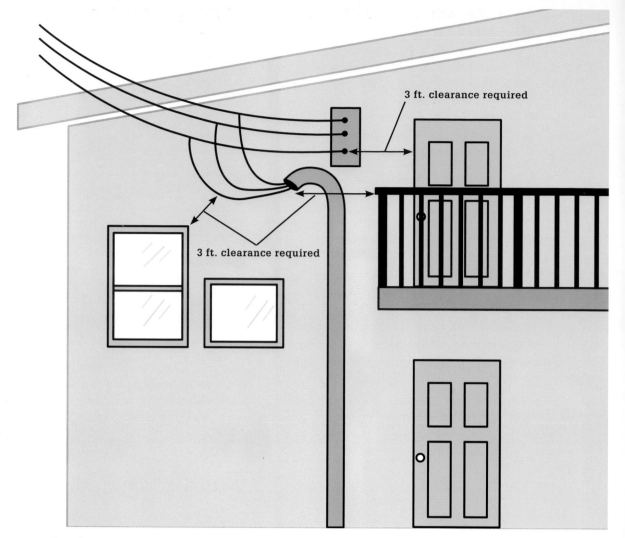

3 ft. clearance required

3 ft. clearance required

Inspect your service clearance to make sure individual service wires are within 3 ft. from doors, operable windows, and decks.

OVERHEAD SERVICE DROP WIRE CLEARANCES

1. Service should provide at least three feet clearance between service drop and service entrance wires and porches, decks, stairs, ladders, fire escapes, balconies, sides of doors, and sides and bottoms of operable windows (not the tops of windows). Clearance should be provided only to service drops and service entrance wires that consist of individual wires and wires that are not protected by a raceway or outer jacket. This means that clearances are usually required for utility service drop wires and are not required for SE type service entrance cable and for wires or cables installed in conduit or tubing.

2. Service should provide at least eight feet vertical clearance between service drop wires and a roof not designed for regular pedestrian traffic with a slope less than four inches in 12 inches.

3. Service should provide at least 10 feet vertical clearance between service drop wires and a roof designed for regular pedestrian traffic. Access to such a roof would usually be by stairs or by a door and the roof edges would be protected by a guard.

4. Service should provide at least three feet vertical clearance between service drop wires and roof with a slope at least four inches in 12 inches.

5. Service should provide at least 18 inches vertical clearance between service drop wires and a roof if:
    (a) the wires pass only over the overhang portion of the roof, and if
    (b) not more than six feet of wire pass over not more than four linear feet of roof surface measured horizontally, and if
    (c) the wires enter a through-the-roof mast or terminate at an approved support.

SERVICE DROP CLEARANCE ABOVE GROUND

1. Measure the vertical clearance between service drop wires and the ground, walkway, driveway, or street beginning at the lowest point of the service drop wires and ending at the surface under the wire's lowest point. The lowest point of the service drop wires is often at the drip loop, but it could be at the point of attachment to the house or it could be where the wires enter the house.
2. Provide at least 10 feet vertical clearance between service drop wires and areas or sidewalks accessed by pedestrians only.
3. Provide at least 12 feet vertical clearance between service drop wires and residential property and driveways.
4. Provide at least 18 feet vertical clearance between service drop wires and public streets, alleys, roads, or parking areas subject to truck traffic.

Safety Tip ▸

If your electrical service entry does not conform to the codes, hire a professional to update it.

The service drop must occur at least 10 ft. above ground level, and as much as 18 ft. in some cases. Occasionally, this means that you must run the conduit for the service mast up through the eave of your roof and seal the roof penetration with a boot.

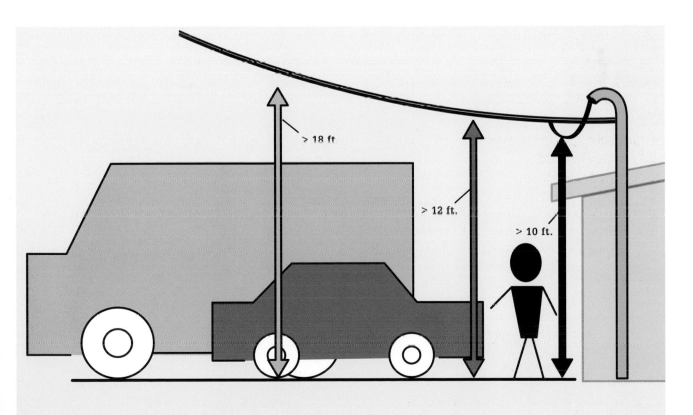

> 18 ft

> 12 ft.

> 10 ft.

Safe clearance between service drop wires and the ground.

Inspect Electrical Panels for Proper Grounding

GROUNDING & BONDING AT SERVICE PANELS AND SUBPANELS

1. The neutral (grounded) wire should be connected to the grounding electrode wire at the nearest accessible point at or before the service equipment (main disconnect). The service equipment is usually the most convenient accessible grounding point because the meter enclosure and points before it are usually locked

Metallic conduit must be physically and electrically connected to panel cabinets. A bonding bushing may be required, in some cases, where all of a knockout is not removed.

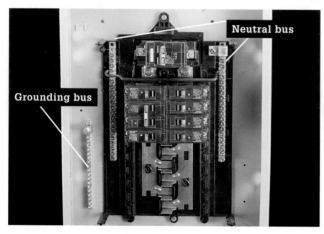

The neutral and grounding wires should not be connected to the same bus in most subpanels. The grounding bus should be bonded to the subpanel cabinet. The neutral bus should not be bonded to the subpanel cabinet.

or secured and not accessible. The grounding electrode wire connects the neutral (grounded) wire to a grounding electrode.

2. The neutral (grounded) wire should not be connected to ground at any other place downstream from the service equipment grounding point. An exception to this rule exists when two buildings are supplied by one electric service.

3. All metal parts of the electrical system should be connected to the neutral (grounded) wire. This includes service equipment and panelboard cases, any metal electrical conduit or tubing, and all metal pipes in the building (such as metal water and gas pipe).

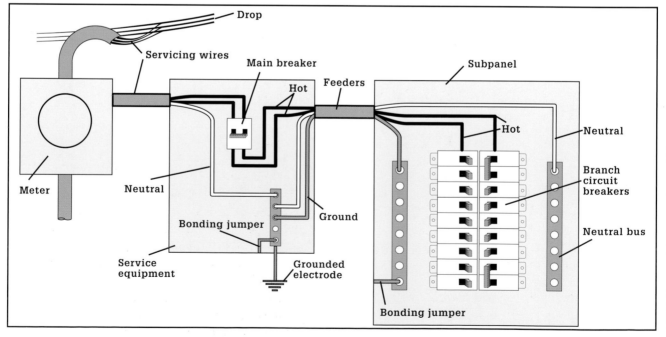

Parts of a common electrical service configuration.

SERVICE GROUNDING AT TWO BUILDINGS USING FOUR-WIRE FEEDER

1. This is the procedure that should be used when installing a new feeder cable to a second building from the building with the primary electric service. This procedure is not required if there is only one branch circuit in the second building and if the new feeder cable contains an equipment grounding wire.

(a) A feeder cable should be installed to the second building that contains an equipment grounding wire. The equipment grounding wire should have been sized as required by International Residential Code Section E3908.

(b) A grounding electrode should be installed at both buildings.

(c) The feeder cable equipment grounding wire should be connected to the grounding electrode wire at the second building subpanel grounding bus. All second building branch circuit equipment grounding wires should be connected to the grounding bus.

(d) The subpanel case should be bonded to the grounding bus.

(e) The feeder cable neutral (grounded) wire should be connected to an isolated grounded bus at the second building subpanel. The grounded bus should not be connected to the subpanel case or to the grounding bus.

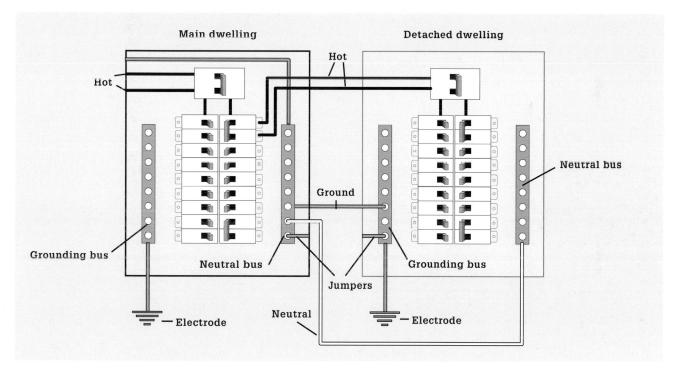

Wiring diagram for wiring a 4-wire feeder from the main service panel to a subpanel in a separate building.

Grounding Electrodes & Electrode Wires

GENERAL REQUIREMENTS

1. Every electrical service should be provided at least one approved type of grounding electrode. The most common grounding electrodes are underground metal water pipe, driven rod and pipe, and concrete encased.

2. All grounding electrodes that may be available at a building should be bonded together. General codes do not require that all possible types of grounding electrodes be installed. They require that if a grounding electrode is installed, it must be connected (bonded) to all other grounding electrodes and to the neutral (grounded) wire.

3. A bonding jumper at least as large as the grounding electrode wire should be used to connect (bond) the grounding electrodes. Bonding jumpers may be connected between grounding electrodes at any convenient point.

4. The grounding electrode wire may be connected at any convenient grounding electrode.

5. Metal underground gas pipe should never be used as a grounding electrode.

Current Wiring Methods

The table "Current Wiring Methods" lists the wiring methods currently allowed in residential construction. Note that certain wiring methods may not be used in certain applications.

APPROVED USES FOR WIRING METHODS

1. The table "Current Wiring Methods Allowed Uses" lists when a wiring method may be used in a specific application. Note that some wiring methods have restrictions or limitations shown by the following superscripts in the table: (1) use less than six feet of LFC if the conduit walls are not reinforced, (2) insulate the neutral (grounded) wire unless the cable is used to supply other buildings on the same property, (3) insulate the neutral (grounded) wire, (4) use wires approved for wet locations and seal raceways to prevent water entry, (5) use materials listed as sunlight resistant, (6) protect metal raceways from corrosion, (7) use Schedule 80 RNC, (8) use materials listed as sunlight resistant if exposed to direct sunlight, (9) use less than six feet of conduit.

Current Wiring Methods ▸

WIRING METHOD	ABBREVIATION
Armored cable	AC
Electrical metallic tubing	EMT
Electrical nonmetallic tubing	ENT
Flexible metal conduit	FMC
Intermediate metal conduit	IMC
Liquidtight flexible conduit	LFC
Metal-clad cable	MC
Nonmetallic sheathed cable	NM
Rigid nonmetallic conduit	RNC
Rigid metallic conduit	RMC
Service entrance cable	SE
Surface raceways	SR
Underground feeder cable	UF
Underground service cable	USE

Current Wiring Methods Allowed Uses ▸

ALLOWED APPLICATION	AC	EMT	ENT	FMC	IMC RMC RNC	LFC[1]	MC	NM	SR	SE	UF	USE
Service entrance	NO	OK	OK[8]	OK[9]	OK	OK[9]	OK	NO	NO	OK	NO	OK
Feeder	OK	OK	OK	OK	OK	OK	OK	OK	NO	OK[2]	OK	OK[2]
Branch circuits	OK	OK	OK	OK	OK	OK	OK	OK	OK	OK[3]	OK	NO
Indoors (e.g., in stud walls)	OK	OK	OK	OK	OK	OK	OK	OK	OK	OK	OK	NO
Wet locations & exposed to sunlight	NO	OK	OK[8]	OK[4]	OK	OK	OK	NO	NO	OK	OK[5]	OK[5]
Damp locations	NO	OK	OK	OK[4]	OK	OK	OK	NO	NO	OK	OK	OK
Embedded in concrete in dry location	NO	OK	OK	NO	OK	NO	NO	NO	NO	NO	NO	NO
Embedded in concrete below grade	NO	OK[6]	OK	NO	OK[6]	NO	NO	NO	NO	NO	NO	NO
Embedded in plaster in dry location	OK	OK	OK	OK	OK	OK	OK	NO	NO	OK	OK	NO
Embedded in masonry	NO	OK	OK	NO	OK[6]	OK	OK	NO	NO	NO	NO	NO
In masonry voids & cells in damp location or below grade	NO	OK[6]	OK	OK[4]	OK[6]	OK	OK	NO	NO	OK	OK	NO
Fished in masonry voids	OK	NO	NO	OK	NO	OK	OK	OK	NO	OK	OK	NO
In masonry voids & cells in dry location	OK	OK	OK	OK	OK	OK	OK	OK	NO	OK	OK	NO
Exposed not subject to damage	OK	OK	OK	OK	OK	OK	OK	OK	OK	OK	OK	OK
Exposed subject to damage	NO	NO	NO	NO	OK[7]	NO	NO	NO	NO	NO	NO	NO
Direct burial	NO	OK[6]	NO	NO	OK[6]	OK	OK[6]	NO	NO	NO	OK	NO

RULES FOR NM CABLE

1. Use table "NM Cable Maximum Ampacity" to determine the maximum ampacity and overcurrent protection of NM cable. NM cable is often referred to by the trade name *Romex*. This table will apply to almost all branch circuit and feeder wiring in modern residential electrical systems. Example: the maximum rating for a circuit breaker protecting Number 12 copper wire is 20 amps.

Rigid metal conduit has threaded ends for making watertight connections with female-threaded fittings and couplings.

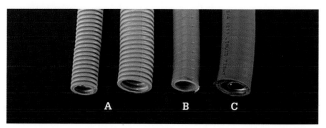

Electrical nonmetallic tubing (A) is an interior-rated material. Liquid-tight flexible conduit can be all nonmetallic (B) or it can be metallic conduit with a nonmetallic sheath (C).

NM Cable Maximum Ampacity ▸

WIRE SIZE (AWG)	COPPER WIRE (AMPS)	ALUMINUM WIRE (AMPS)
14	15	–
12	20	15
10	30	25
8	40	30
6	55	40
4	70	55
3	85	65
2	95	75
1	110	85

Nonmetallic sheathed cable is available in the most common gauges used in residential construction.

Maximum Hole or Notch Size in Studs and Joists ▸

FRAMING MEMBER	MAXIMUM HOLE SIZE	MAXIMUM NOTCH SIZE
2 × 4 load-bearing stud	1⁷⁄₁₆" diameter	⁷⁄₈" deep
2 × 4 nonload bearing stud	2⅛" diameter	1⁷⁄₁₆" deep
2 × 6 load-bearing stud	2¼" diameter	1⅜" deep
2 × 6 nonload-bearing stud	3⁵⁄₁₆" diameter	2³⁄₁₆" deep
2 × 6 joists	1⅞" diameter	⁷⁄₈" deep
2 × 8 joists	2⅜" diameter	1¼" deep
2 × 10 joists	3¹⁄₁₆" diameter	1½" deep
2 × 12 joists	3¾" diameter	1⅞" deep

This framing member chart shows the maximum sizes for holes and notches that can be cut into studs and joists when running cables. When boring holes, there must be at least ⅝" of wood between the edge of a stud and the hole, and at least 2" between the edge of a joist and the hole. Joists can be notched only in the end ⅓ of the overall span, never in the middle ⅓ of the joist.

NM & UF CABLE INSTALLATION

1. Use NM and UF cable where the cable is not subject to physical damage. Physical damage can occur unless the cable is covered by drywall or other material or unless the cable is run in conduit or tubing. Physical damage includes damage by sunlight.

2. Protect NM and UF cable using RMC, IMC, EMT, or Schedule 80 RNC when the cable is subject to physical damage. Extend the protection at least six inches above the floor when the cable runs through the floor. This provision applies to exposed wall framing, such as unfinished basements and garages, and to cable that runs through framed and concrete slab floors. This provision does not apply to cable run in attics and in basement ceiling joists.

3. Protect NM and UF cable using nail guards or other approved physical protection when the cable is installed:
    (a) through holes, notches, or grooves that are closer than 1¼ inches to the edge of a stud or joist,
    (b) in notches and grooves in places such as drywall, plaster, and under carpet, unless the groove or notch is deeper than 1¼ inches,
    (c) through holes in metal framing (use grommets or bushings), and
    (d) parallel to the edge of a stud, joist, or furring strip when the cable is closer than 1¼ inches to the edge of the framing member.

4. Support NM and UF cable every 4½ feet. Use wire staples or other approved fasteners to secure vertical runs of NM and UF cable. Staple the cable only on the flat edge. NM and UF cable run across the tops of joists is usually considered supported.

5. Secure NM and UF cable not more than 8 inches from boxes and terminations that do not have cable clamps. This includes most plastic boxes. Secure NM and UF cable not more than 12 inches from boxes and terminations that have cable clamps. This includes most metal boxes. Measure the support distance from where the cable sheathing ends in the box, not from the box itself.

6. Use NM cable only in dry locations that are indoors and not within concrete or masonry that is exposed to the ground. Do not use NM cable in conduit that is buried in the ground. Buried conduit is considered a wet location. You may use UF cable in wet locations including outdoors and underground if it is not subject to damage.

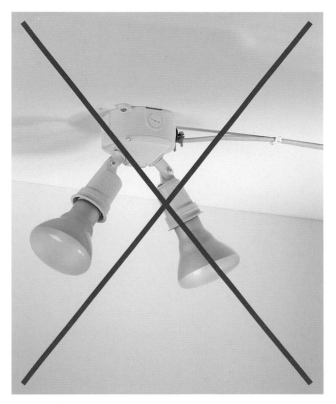

VIOLATION! Do not install NM and UF cable on drywall.

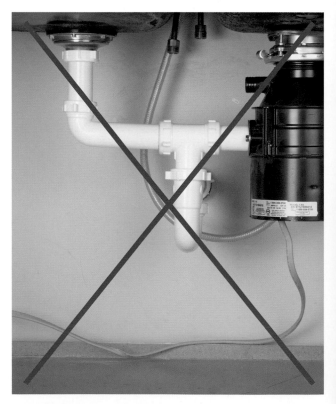

VIOLATION! Do not install NM and UF cable inside cabinets.

VIOLATION! Do not install NM and UF cable in exposed walls and ceilings. You may install NM and UF cable in exposed basement ceilings and attics under certain conditions.

VIOLATION! Do not install NM cable outdoors. Outdoors includes buried conduit. You may install UF cable outdoors if it is protected from physical damage.

Support NM and UF cable at least every 4½ ft. Cable on top of ceiling joists is considered supported.

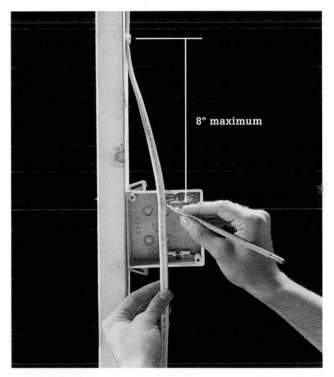

8" maximum

Secure NM and UF cable within 8" from where the cable enters or leaves a plastic box. Measure from where the cable sheathing ends in the box, not from the edge of the box.

Electrical Receptacle Installation

Whether you call them outlets, plug-ins, or receptacles, these important devices represent the point where the rubber meets the road in your home wiring system. From the basic 15-amp, 120-volt duplex receptacle to the burly 50-amp, 240-volt appliance receptacle, the many outlets in your home do pretty much the same thing: transmit power to a load.

Learning the essential differences between receptacles does not take long. Amperage is the main variable, as each receptacle must match the amperage and voltage of the circuit in which it is installed. A 15-amp circuit should be wired with 15-amp receptacles; a 20-amp circuit needs 20-amp receptacles (identified by the horizontal slot that Ts into each tall polarized slot). A 20-amp multi-receptacle circuit may use either 15- or 20-amp receptacles. Receptacles for 240-volt service have unique slot configurations so you can't accidentally plug in an appliance that's not rated for the amperage in the circuit. Some receptacles can be wired using the push-in wire holes, but this is not recommended. Some receptacles provide built-in, ground-fault circuit protection, tripping the circuit breaker if there is a short circuit or power surge. These are easy to identify by reset and test buttons.

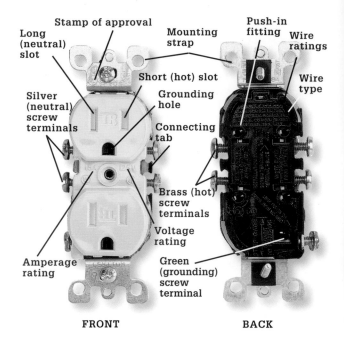

FRONT   BACK

RECEPTACLE INSTALLATION IN ROOMS

1. Apply these provisions to receptacles in living rooms, family rooms, bedrooms, dens, sunrooms, recreation rooms, dining rooms, breakfast rooms, libraries, and similar living areas. Kitchens, bathrooms, hallways, garages, laundry rooms, and exterior receptacles have their own installation requirements.

2. Install the required interior receptacles so that any point along a wall is not more than six feet from a receptacle. Do not include operable doors, fireplaces, closet interiors, and similar openings when measuring a wall. A wall begins at the edge of an opening and continues around any corners to the next opening. Walls include fixed (not sliding) panels in doors that are at least two feet wide. Walls include partial height walls that serve functions such as room dividers and walls that form breakfast bars and similar bar-type counters. Walls include guards and railings at balconies, raised floors, and other areas where furniture could be placed.

3. Locate floor receptacles intended to serve as required interior receptacles not more than 18 inches from the wall. You may install interior floor receptacles at any safe place, but you may count only receptacles not more than 18 inches from the wall among the required receptacles.

4. Install receptacles not more than 66 inches above the finished floor. You may install receptacles at any height, but you may count only receptacles not more than 66 inches above the finished floor among the required receptacles.

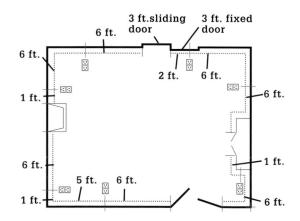

Example of receptacle spacing requirements in a typical room. Measure receptacle spacing distance along the wall line. Install receptacles along partial height walls and along balcony guards in lofts and similar areas.

KITCHEN COUNTERTOP RECEPTACLE INSTALLATION

1. Install a GFCI protected receptacle at every kitchen countertop that is at least 12 inches wide.

2. Install kitchen countertop receptacles so that all points along the countertop wall are not more than two feet from a receptacle. A wall begins at the edge of an opening or appliance and continues around any corners and ends at the next opening or appliance. Include windows when measuring the wall unless the window is above a sink or cooking appliance.

3. Install receptacles behind a sink or cooking appliance located along a straight wall if the countertop behind the sink or cooking appliance is at least 12 inches wide. Install receptacles behind a sink or cooking appliance located along a wall corner if the countertop behind the sink or cooking appliance is at least 18 inches wide.

4. Install receptacles not more than 20 inches above the countertop. You may install receptacles at any height, but you may include only receptacles not more than 20 inches above the countertop among the required kitchen countertop receptacles.

5. Do not include among the required kitchen countertop receptacles:
   (a) receptacles located in appliance garages, and
   (b) receptacles dedicated for a fixed-in-place appliance, and
   (c) receptacles not readily accessible for use by small appliances.

6. Do not install receptacles face up on work surfaces.

You must install receptacles behind a short run of countertop if it is at least 12" wide along a straight wall.

You must install receptacles behind a sink or cooking appliance if the countertop behind the sink or cooking appliance is at least 18" wide in a corner cabinet.

Safety Tip ▸

Always shut off power at the main service panel before inspection, repairing, or installing receptacles.

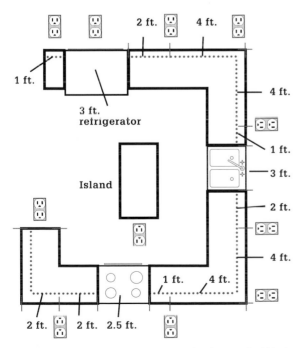

Example of countertop receptacle spacing in a typical kitchen.

Ground-fault (GFCI) & Arc-fault (AFCI) Protection

GROUND-FAULT LOCATION REQUIREMENTS

1. Kitchen. Install ground-fault circuit interrupt (GFCI) protection on all 120-volt receptacles that serve kitchen countertops. This does not include receptacles under the kitchen sink and receptacles located on kitchen walls that do not serve the countertop.

2. Bathroom. Install ground-fault circuit interrupt (GFCI) protection on all 120-volt receptacles located in bathrooms. This applies to all receptacles regardless of where they are located in the bathroom and includes receptacles located at countertops, inside cabinets, and along bathroom walls. Install ground-fault circuit interrupt (GFCI) protection on all circuits serving electrically heated floors in bathrooms.

3. Garage and Accessory Building Receptacles. Install ground-fault circuit interrupt (GFCI) protection on all 120-volt receptacles located in garages and grade-level areas of unfinished accessory buildings. You do not need to provide GFCI protection for receptacles that are not readily accessible such as receptacles in the garage ceiling. You

do not need to provide GFCI protection for dedicated receptacles that serve an appliance that is not easily moved. Examples of dedicated receptacles include receptacles for water softeners, refrigerators, alarm systems, and central vacuums. The receptacle must be a single receptacle when serving a single appliance or a duplex receptacle if serving two appliances. A duplex receptacle serving one appliance is a violation.

4. Exterior receptacles. Install ground-fault circuit interrupt (GFCI) protection on all 120-volt receptacles located outdoors. This does not apply to receptacles that are dedicated for deicing equipment and are located under the eaves. This applies to holiday lighting receptacles located under the eaves.

5. Basement receptacles. Install ground-fault circuit interrupt (GFCI) protection on all 120-volt receptacles located in unfinished basements. An unfinished basement is not intended as habitable space and is limited to storage and work space. The exceptions for garage receptacles apply to unfinished basement receptacles.

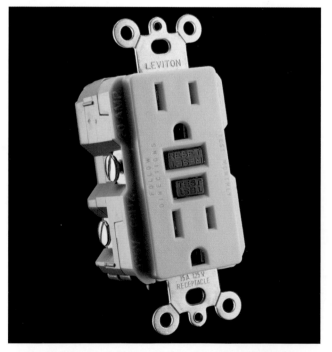

Ground-fault receptacles and circuit breakers detect unwanted current running between an energized wire and a grounded wire.

A combination ARC-fault circuit breaker detects sparking (arcing) faults along damaged energized wires and detects these faults between wires. A branch ARC-fault circuit breaker only detects arcing faults between wires. Use only combination ARC-fault circuit breakers in new work and when replacing old ARC-fault breakers.

6. Crawl space receptacles. Install ground-fault circuit interrupt (GFCI) protection on all 120-volt receptacles located in crawl spaces. Receptacles in crawl spaces are not required unless equipment requiring service is located there.

7. Laundry, utility, and bar sink receptacles. Install ground-fault circuit interrupt (GFCI) protection on all 120-volt receptacles that are located within six feet of the outside edge of a laundry, utility, or bar sink. This includes wall, floor, and countertop receptacles. This includes any appliance receptacles within the six feet distance, such as the washing machine receptacle.

8. Boathouse receptacles. Install ground-fault circuit interrupt (GFCI) protection on all 120-volt receptacles located in boathouses.

9. Spas, tubs, and other circuits requiring ground-fault protection. Install ground-fault circuit interrupt (GFCI) protection on all circuits serving spa tubs, whirlpool tubs, hot tubs, and similar equipment. Refer to the general codes for more information about receptacles serving these components.

ARC-FAULT LOCATION REQUIREMENTS

1. Install an arc-fault circuit interrupter (AFCI) on each 120-volt branch circuit serving bedrooms. This means that lighting, smoke alarm, receptacle, and any other bedroom outlets must be AFCI protected. Install the AFCI at the origination of the branch circuit.

2. Use only combination type AFCI after January 1, 2008.

3. You may install the AFCI not more than six feet from the origination of the branch circuit if you run the wires in metal conduit or a metallic sheath. Measure the six feet along the branch circuit wires.

4. Note that the 2008 National Electrical Code (NEC) requires AFCI protection for all 15- and 20-amp branch circuits. This requirement is controversial and may not be adopted in every jurisdiction. Verify local adoption of the 2008 NEC requirement with your local building official.

Receptacles for whirlpool tubs must be GFCI protected.

Junction Boxes, Device Boxes & Enclosures

All electrical boxes are available in different depths. A box must be deep enough so a switch or receptacle can be removed or installed easily without crimping and damaging the circuit wires. Replace an undersized box with a larger box using the Electrical Box Fill Chart (see page 124) as a guide. **The NEC also says that all electrical boxes must remain accessible. Never cover an electrical box with drywall, paneling, or wall coverings.**

NONMETALLIC BOX INSTALLATION

1. Use nonmetallic boxes only with NM type cable or with nonmetallic conduit or tubing. You may use nonmetallic boxes with metallic conduit or tubing if you maintain the electrical continuity of the metallic conduit or tubing by installing a bonding jumper through the box. In many situations it is easier to use a metallic box with metallic conduit or tubing.
2. Extend NM cable sheathing at least ¼ inch into a nonmetallic box knockout opening.
3. Secure NM cable, conduit, and tubing to each box. You may secure NM cable with cable clamps inside the box or with compression tabs provided where the cable enters the box. You do not need to secure NM cable to a standard single-gang box (2¼ by four inches) mounted in a wall or ceiling if you fasten the cable not more than eight inches from the box and if the sheathing enters the box at least ¼ inch. Measure the eight inches along the length of the sheathing, not from the outside of the box.

LIGHT FIXTURE BOX INSTALLATION

1. Use boxes designed for mounting light fixtures if a light fixture is to be mounted to the box. These boxes are usually four-inch round or octagonal. You may use other boxes if the light fixture weighs not more than six pounds and is secured to the box using at least two #6 or larger screws.
2. Support light fixtures weighing at least 50 pounds independently from the light fixture box. You may use the light fixture box to support light fixtures weighing less than 50 pounds. Note that ceiling fans are not light fixtures.

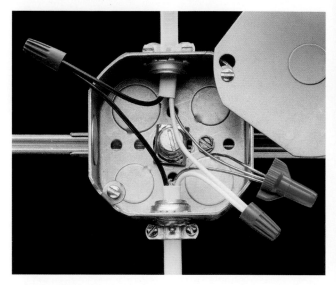

Box shape is directly related to function, as electrical fixtures are created to fit on boxes of a particular shape. Octagonal and round boxes generally are designed for ceiling mounting, while square and rectangular boxes are sized for single-pole, duplex, and other standard switch and receptacle sizes.

Do not support heavy light fixtures using only the light fixture electrical box. The eye hook supporting this chandelier is driven into the same ceiling joist to which the electrical box is mounted.

BOX CONTENTS LIMITATIONS

1. Limit the number of wires, devices (such as switches and receptacles), and fittings in a box. This limitation is primarily based on the heat generated by the wires and devices in the box. The actual size of the box relative to its contents is a secondary consideration.
2. Use the cubic inch volume printed on the box or provided in the box manufacturer's instructions to determine box volume. Do not attempt to measure the box volume. Do not estimate box volume from the volume of similar size boxes. You will probably not get the same volume as provided by the manufacturer.
3. Use table "Wire Volume Unit" to determine the volume units required by wires, devices, and fittings in a box.

BOX INSTALLATION TOLERANCES

1. Install boxes in non-combustible material, such as masonry, so that the front edge is not more than ¼ inch from the finished surface.
2. Install boxes in walls and ceilings made of wood or other combustible material so that the front edge is flush with the finished surface or projects from the finished surface.
3. Cut openings for boxes in drywall and plaster so that the opening is not more than ⅛ inch from the perimeter of the box.

Boxes must be installed so the front edges are flush with the finished wall surface, and the gap between the box and the wall covering is not more than ⅛".

Wire Volume Unit ▸

WIRE SIZE (AWG)	WIRE VOLUME
18	1.50 in.³
16	1.75 in.³
14	2.00 in.³
12	2.25 in.³
10	2.50 in.³
8	3.00 in.³
6	5.00 in.³

Volume Units ▸

Calculate the volume units required by wires, devices, and fittings based on the following definitions:

Volume units for current-carrying wires. Allow one volume unit for each individual hot (ungrounded) and neutral (grounded) wire in the box. Use Table 47 to determine the volume units of common wire sizes. Example: two pieces of #14/2 NM are in a box. Each piece of this cable contains one hot (ungrounded) and one neutral (grounded) wire and one grounding wire. From table "Wire Volume Unit", each #14 wire uses 2.00 cubic inches in the box. The total volume units required by the hot (ungrounded) and neutral (grounded) wires is eight cubic inches.

Volume units for devices. Allow two volume units for each device (switch or receptacle) in the box. Base the volume units on the largest hot (ungrounded) or neutral (grounded) wire in the box. Example: NM cable size #14 and #12 are in a

box. From Table 47, #14 wire uses 2.00 cubic inches and #12 wire uses 2.25 cubic inches. Allow 4.5 cubic inches volume units (2 × 2.25 cubic inches) for each switch or receptacle in the box based on the volume of the larger #12 NM cable.

Volume units for grounding wires. Allow one volume unit for all grounding wires in the box. Base the volume unit on the largest hot (ungrounded) or neutral (grounded) wire in the box.

Volume units for clamps. Allow one volume unit for all internal cable clamps in the box, if any. Base the volume unit on the largest hot (ungrounded) or neutral (grounded) wire in the box.

Volume units for fittings. Allow one volume unit for all fittings in the box, if any. Base the volume unit on the largest hot (ungrounded) or neutral (grounded) wire in the box.

Electrical Box Fill Chart ▸

BOX SIZE AND SHAPE	MAXIMUM NUMBER OF VOLUME UNITS PERMITTED (SEE NOTES BELOW)			
(If volume not labeled by manufacturer)	14 AWG	12 AWG	10 AWG	8 AWG
JUNCTION BOXES				
4 × 1¼" R or O	6	5	5	4
4 × 1½" R or O	7	6	6	5
4 × 2⅛" R or O	10	9	8	7
4 × 1¼" S	9	8	7	6
4 × 1½" S	10	9	8	7
4 × 2⅛" S	15	13	12	10
4¹¹⁄₁₆ × 1¼" S	12	11	10	8
4¹¹⁄₁₆ × 1½" S	14	13	11	9
4¹¹⁄₁₆ × 2⅛" S	21	18	16	14
DEVICE BOXES				
3 × 2 × 1½"	3	3	3	2
3 × 2 × 2"	5	4	4	3
3 × 2 × 2¼"	5	4	4	3
3 × 2 × 2½"	6	5	5	4
3 × 2 × 2¾"	7	6	6	4
3 × 2 × 3½"	9	8	7	6
4 × 2⅛ × 1½"	5	4	4	3
4 × 2⅛ × 1⅞"	6	5	5	4
4 × 2⅛ × 2⅛"	7	6	5	4

Notes:
- R = Round; O = Octagonal; S = Square or rectangular
- Each hot or neutral wire entering the box is counted as one volume unit
- Grounding wires are counted as one volume unit in total—do not count each one individually.
- Raceway fittings and external cable clamps do not count. Internal cable connectors and straps count as one volume unit.
- Devices (switches and receptacles mainly) each count as two volume units.
- When calculating total volume units, any non-wire components should be assigned the gauge of the largest wire in the box.
- For wire gauges not shown here, contact your local electrical inspections office.

BOX SUPPORT IN WALLS, CEILINGS & FLOORS

1. Provide support for boxes that rigidly and securely fasten them in place. You may use nails or screws to support these boxes.
2. Protect screws inside boxes so that the threads will not damage the wires.
3. Wood braces used to support boxes must be at least one by two inches.
4. Use "cut-in" or "old work" retrofit boxes only if they have approved clamps or anchors that are identified for the location where they are installed.

DAMP LOCATIONS

1. Install a receptacle box cover that is weatherproof when the cover is closed and a plug is not inserted into a receptacle located in a damp location. This applies to 15-amp and 20-amp receptacles. A damp area is protected from direct contact with water. Refer to the definition of damp location. You may use a receptacle cover suitable for wet locations in a damp location.
2. Install a watertight seal between a flush-mounted receptacle and its faceplate. This will require a gasket or sealant between the finished surface (such as stucco, brick, or siding) and the faceplate.

WET LOCATIONS

1. Install a receptacle box cover that is weatherproof when the cover is closed on any receptacle located in a wet location. This applies to 15-amp and 20-amp receptacles in any indoor or outdoor wet location. This applies regardless of whether or not a plug is inserted into the receptacle.
2. Install a watertight seal between a flush-mounted receptacle and its faceplate. This will require a gasket or sealant between the finished surface (such as stucco, brick, or siding) and the faceplate.

Resources & Photo Credits

Applied Energy Innovations
Solar, wind, geothermal installations
612-532-0384
www.appliedenergyinnovations.org

Black & Decker
Portable power tools and more
www.blackanddecker.com

Broan-NuTone, LLC
Vent fans
800-558-1711
www.broan.com

Generac Power Systems
Standby generators and switches
www.generac.com
www.guardiangenerators.com

**Honda Power Equipment/
American Honda Motor Company, Inc.**
Standby generators
678-339-2600
www.hondapowerequipment.com

Kohler
Standby generators
800-4-Kohler
www.kohlerco.com

Pass & Seymour Legrand
Home automation products
800-223-4185
www.passandseymour.com

Red Wing Shoes Co.
Work shoes and boots shown throughout book
800-733-9464
www.redwingshoes.com

Unistrut Metal Framing
Solar panel mounts
800-521-7730
www.unistrut.com

Westinghouse
Ceiling fans, decorative lighting, solar outdoor
    lighting, & other lighting fixtures and bulbs
800-245-5874
Purchase here: www.budgetlighting.com
www.westinghouse.com

Index

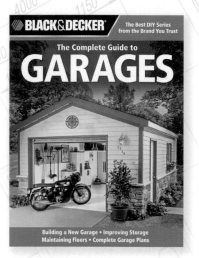
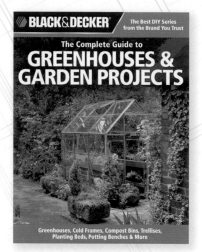
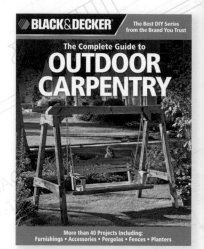

WORKBENCH
Reference Card

Wire Color Chart

Wire color		Function
	White	Neutral wire carrying current at zero voltage.
	Black	Hot wire carrying current at full voltage.
	Red	Hot wire carrying current at full voltage.
	White, colored markings	Hot wire carrying current at full voltage.
	Green	Serves as a grounding pathway.
	Bare copper	Serves as a grounding pathway.

Wire Size Chart

Wire gauge		Wire capacity & use
	#6	60 amps, 240 volts; central air conditioner, electric furnace.
	#8	40 amps, 240 volts; electric range, central air conditioner.
	#10	30 amps, 240 volts; window air conditioner, clothes dryer.
	#12	20 amps, 120 volts; light fixtures, receptacles, microwave oven.
	#14	15 amps, 120 volts; light fixtures, receptacles.
	#16	Light-duty extension cords.
	#18 to 22	Thermostats, doorbells, security systems.

ADVANCED WIRING
Current with 2012-2015 Codes

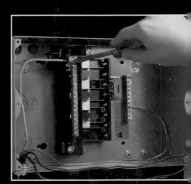

Wire Like a Pro

Wiring is never easy, but even advanced projects can be achieved with sound instruction. That's where *Advanced Home Wiring* comes in. Hiring a professional to handle your total wiring needs can cost a few hundred dollars or more; with this guide, you'll keep your attention on your project and not on your pocket book.

In this updated 3rd edition, you'll find an all-new troubleshooting guide for safe solutions when your wires get crossed. We'll teach you how to upgrade a main service panel from 100 to 200 amps, and show you firsthand how to rewire your dream kitchen. You'll even find instructions on how to ground and bond an updated electrical system, and how to use diagnostic wiring tools. Become your own home wiring expert with Black and Decker's *Advanced Home Wiring*.

THIS BOOK INCLUDES:

- 28 common circuit maps
- How to upgrade a service panel
- Solar circuit installation
- Troubleshooting and repairs

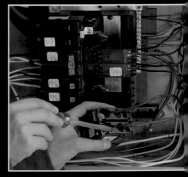

Tools & Materials lists
Know what you will need for each project before you begin

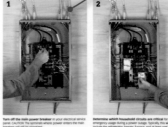

Over 300 photos and Illustrations
Navigate each step of the project quickly and easily

Detailed step-by-step Instructions
Never have to guess about what to do next

CATEGORY: HOME IMPROVEMENT

$18.99 US
£14.99 UK
$20.99 CAN

Creative Publishing
international
www.creativepub.com
1-800-328-0590 opt. 2

ISBN – 13: 978-1-58923-702-5